What is the Alt-Right?

By M Taylors

First Paperback Edition

ISBN-13: 978-1541228559

ISBN-10: 1541228553

10 9 8 7 6 5 4 3 2 1

realmtaylors@gmail.com

@realMTaylors

Contents

"The demographics of the country are going to change. It's inevitable.

The Latino community in America is going to grow. If you stopped all immigration today, just by virtue of birth rates, this is going to be a browner country."

Barack Obama, NPR, December 15, 2016

1

The pro-white sphere.

The alt-right is like all movements in the fact that it fits into groups with undesirable beliefs. Conservatism is right-wing, but so is Nazism. Liberalism is left wing, but it shares that label with communism. The alt-right is a white identity movement, so being a white movement instantly puts the alt-right under an umbrella with "undesirable" sections.

Everyone has heard of the Ku Klux Klan and everyone has heard of white supremacists, but most would say that they have never actually met one. One may see them in the news or a perhaps see a few racist remarks in the comment section on the Internet, but the interaction stops there.[1] The alt-right falls somewhere in between the aforementioned and the most conservative members of Congress, albeit they may fall closer to the former. The alt-right fits into the pro-white movement, which inevitably leads to comparisons with the KKK and other hate groups, but pro-black movements, along with every other movement, have acceptable views which obviously end up also being held by extremists. Just look at the Green Party of literally every country.

Like many ventures, the first time I encountered the pro-white movement's stream of ideas was on accident and had innocent beginnings. In 2012 I became quite fascinated with animal behavior and the effects of one species on the environment and on other species. Introducing a species of plant or animal into another environment, continent, or country typically takes on an unexpected transformation of the ecosystem. Sometimes a type of plant or animal moving itself (or being taken) to another place where it had previously not existed does not change much, but sometimes the introduction of a new species has a tremendous effect on the local biological life. In the case of an animal, breeding quickly and outnumbering local species can cause devastation to other animals and even plant life. Certain plants can also have such catastrophic effects on their new environment.

This interest led me to learning about critically endangered species of animal and I had the idea that if I could somehow acquire some, I would be able to breed them until their population had risen once again. I often search for things like "Recent extinct animals" or "Animals closest to becoming extinct."

One day I was sitting at my computer and wondered, *Will white people go extinct?* I typed my question into the search bar and clicked on a video. I remember seeing a pie chart with slices representing different races or ethnicities of people.[2] The video went through the past, present, and future, showing slides of the world's racial demographics over the years. Slices representing non-whites increased and the absolute numbers increased for each group. The white slice got smaller and smaller, going from about one third to about one fifteenth and being the only group to lose people.

I had to do more digging, so I watched more videos and saw more statistics, but I wondered if the numbers were all being made up. After researching total fertility rates (the rate of births occurring in a group) and population projections, I concluded that the original video was essentially accurate. Due to my earlier interest in the growth and decline of nonhuman, biological life, my interest transitioned over quite easily. I started researching the demographics of continents and specific countries, immigration trends, fertility trends, and population growth.

This was the first time I came across an explicitly pro-white person on the web. Teutonic Warrior Chick (who also goes by other names) made videos on Youtube criticizing minorities, President Obama, and oftentimes Jews. Most of her videos were brightly lit during filming, emphasizing her white skin with a bright shine. I found it quite interesting to listen to what a person like her thought about the current events and how she viewed them through the lens of "White Genocide," a supposed event taking place with almost no one noticing. As a conservative, I listened to her criticize the President and liberals, but I brushed off the Jewish comments she made. This eventually led me to questioning her logic. White people are supposedly being erased, but Jews are white too, right?

I searched "Are Jews White" and that led me to a message board called Stormfront. The site is for white people to chat and discuss topics concerning mainly race and politics. It was made by Don Black, a former member of the KKK and the National Socialist White People's Party.[3] The site's user base is mainly compose of neo-

Nazis, white nationalists, "alt-righters," or just plain old racists. During the time I watched the white nationalist sphere of the Internet, I also kept an eye on the black nationalists to a lesser extent. Now back to my question on whether Jews are white. The simple answer was "No," but there are interesting reasons they gave as to why.

Firstly, let us note that most would say Middle Easterners, including Jews, and North Africans (Egyptians, Libyans, etc.) are not black or Asian, so that leaves Caucasian. Generally, Americans of European descent (Swedish, English, German, French, etc.), would not consider Middle Easterners and Libyans to be white. They might not even consider Spaniards or Italians to be white. Take out a map and look at Spain and Italy's bordering countries. They both share a border with France and Italy is also touching Switzerland. So they are white (European), but are Jews white? They are not European, and those on the alt-right would say that is a requirement to be white. For the rest of this book, "white" means "Europeans, including Russians."[4] Look at the map again and move from Europe to Israel. First you get to Turkey, then Syria, and then perhaps hop through Lebanon if that would be your preference. The Turks, Syrians, and

Lebanese are not white. Logic would dictate Jews are not white.

What about Jews like Natalie Portman and Zac Efron, who look white and are probably more white than Jewish? The alt-right's definition of white would be wholly European, and in the case someone might be one-sixteenth non-white, "...If a person identifies with his non-White part so much that he is concerned about it and feels compelled to tell us about it, then we consider him to be non-White."[5] That quote comes from Stormfront and may be the strictest definition, but many on the (less extreme) alt-right would actually allow someone who is a sixteenth non-white if it is not visible or spoken of. There can even be a difference if the person is a fourth Egyptian, for instance, or a fourth black, because Egyptians are genetically closer to whites than blacks are. Sometimes someone who is a fourth Egyptian would be more accepted than someone who is an eighth black. Usually if the person is mainly white, appears white, identifies as white, and acts white, then that is acceptable. If one has an amount of non-white in them, identifying with it is not acceptable. This is one reason Jews are not considered white: they usually identify more with Israel than Europe.

After all, according to American Jews, the most important aspect of being Jewish is remembering the Holocaust.[6] That's a crucial historical and cultural difference between Jews and whites. As for someone who still wonders, "Does the alt-right want people to undergo DNA testing to prove they are white?" the simple answer the alt-right would give is, "Israel can demand DNA tests for immigrants to prove they are Jewish,[7] so we could ask for DNA tests also."

Like the definition of the alt-right being slightly flexible, the racial standard also has a little wiggle room. One may say that there is no way a movement can be successful if they cannot even identify their potential members, but an alt-righter would simply point out that leftists and minorities have no problem defining "white" when it comes to blaming white people for slavery or another injustice. The people in these movements have a lot to say and after listening to them for a long time and hearing them say something like the abovementioned, you realize there are indeed a lot of things that you haven't thought of before. Black American journalists write about how they give their children the race "talk," but whites in America usually ignore the topic altogether.

If a white American does have the chance to listen to discussions on race, it is either a liberal explaining "white privilege" and how disadvantaged minorities are, or a conservative informing them why that is false. There is rarely a time when the pendulum swings toward the position that says whites are the victims unless it is something ridiculous like affirmative action. It never gets down to the nitty-gritty when it comes to crime, IQ, or other taboo topics intersecting with race.

Now, none of the individuals I have mentioned actually called themselves alt-right, but something further to the right. A short time after Youtube or Teutonic Warrior Chick deleted her videos,[8] although some were reuploaded by others, was when I first learned of the alt-right.

The first time I saw the term "alt-right" was the name of a Twitter user, @_Altright_. Due to the writing style and tweets, he appeared to be a man, in spite of having the picture of Marion Maréchal-Le Pen, a French politician who is regularly praised in alt-right circles. His account was created in 2010, being perhaps the oldest alt-right Twitter celebrity and even having over 15,000 followers. For the next few months I regularly checked his tweets because he seemed like the most realistic person, in spite of also appearing idealistic. He tweeted out thoughts on current events and often humorous ideas, along with motivational pictures for his followers. It was interesting to watch people call him racist and to see how he would respond, especially when there were "drunk tweets." He was not as extreme as some "white supremacists" I knew of on the Internet, but he was definitely no moderate. I believe that his views and tweets represent most of what the alt-right stands for. The alt-right believes that it is right, and it is passionate about its goals even if people will denounce it and shout it down. The alt-right is resolute.

2

Emergence of the alt-right.

Richard Spencer is an American who has made his way from Massachusetts to Texas and from Montana to Virginia. Spencer coined the term "alternative right" in August 2008,[1] but some attribute its creation to Paul Gottfried when he gave a speech in November 2008.[2] Like most new terms, Spencer's did not take off until years later, peaking in prominence in the current year of 2016. This expansion was fueled by much of the same events that led to the rise of Donald Trump, and this became a symbiotic relationship between Trump and the alt-right.

The alt-right, as a pro-white movement, blossomed in the light of Trump because he was the only candidate that held strong views that just seemed to give them hope: build a wall, deport illegal aliens, end the anchor baby policy, stop allowing immigrants to come into America while Americans are unemployed, choose immigrants who are likely to succeed, and select immigrants from Europe.[3] All of these policies are pro-white, but they are also supported by many conservatives who do not actually say it. That is why Trump energized the alt-right: he said it. The alt-right's enthusiasm surrounding these issues brought Trump through the primaries and Trump, by becoming the Republican nominee, brought the alt-right into the public eye.

One of the first published pieces of this election cycle concerning the alt-right was written by Rosie Gray,[4] but the first *mainstream* article arrived in March 2016 by Milo Yiannopoulos and Allum Bokhari of Breitbart. Gray still remains the journalist who covers the alt-right the most, but Yiannopoulos, being a flamboyant television personality with connections and already having a wide base of fans, was the one who shined the spotlight on the alt-right. The article by Yiannopoulos/Bokhari "explains" that

> ...The alt-right openly crack[s] jokes about the Holocaust, loudly — albeit almost entirely satirically — expresses its horror at "race-mixing," and denounces the

"degeneracy" of homosexuals...
while inviting Jewish gays and
mixed-race Breitbart reporters to
their secret dinner parties. What
gives?

...It's just about having fun.
They have no real problem with
race-mixing, homosexuality, or
even diverse societies: it's just fun
to watch the mayhem and outrage
that erupts when those secular
shibboleths are openly mocked.[5]

What "secret" dinner parties are you talking
about, Yiannopoulos? Most of the higher-ups in the alt-
right don't know you and don't necessarily like you.[6] This
explanation by Breitbart's writers is one of the reasons
people are so confused about what the alt-right wants
and what it means. He says he is not alt-right, but then
says they are just an elaborate prank. If they are just a
joke, he likes to be outrageous like them, he holds most
of their "non-joking" views, and he goes to their secret

dinner parties, why not be alt-right himself? He avoids the label because it is not a joke and he is not one of them.

These types of representations increase the muddiness surrounding the term. News station workers think *Who should I invite on my show to discuss the alt-right?* They then proceed to search for "alt-right" on the Internet and find either a liberal blogger who thinks alt-righters are Nazis or a libertarian (Yiannopoulos) who thinks they are kids making jokes. Writers or journalists do, indeed, ask actual alt-right people for interviews, but it is difficult for the public to make a connection with people when the writer wields the pen of portrayal and chooses how to frame the interview. Radio and television shows are specifically avoiding interviewing eloquent, alt-right guests that might make arguments the hosts never had to face, hence lacking a response to any points made. They cannot take the risk of looking stupid. As I have mentioned earlier, most don't discuss (or know how to safely navigate the discussion of) crime, IQ, or other touchy topics intersecting with race.

Additionally, common sense says a person would more likely investigate the alt-right if they actually listened to or watched someone, rather than reading a passage from them. Most radio and television hosts do not want their fans to start researching topics like the alt-right, and they do not want their fans complaining about inviting "evil" people onto their shows or giving them a platform to spread their "bigoted" ideas. Now whenever someone sees Yiannopoulos on television discussing the alt-right, they search his name and end up never making it past him.[7]

After these few alt-right interviews and interactions in the press, the ultimate event that cemented the alt-right into American politics was a campaign speech by Hillary Clinton in Reno, Nevada, on the 25th of August, 2016, which she was almost 2 hours late for.[8] MSNBC discussed the alt-right the day before Clinton's speech and a personality explained that it is a very tech-savvy, sexist brand of white nationalism more resembling European politics than America's.[9] That would be true, except you need to subtract the sexism and inject some humor.

The alt-right looked forward to this speech and anticipated vast numbers of people searching the Internet for "What is the alt-right?" They planned accordingly by posting a host of videos entitled exactly that.[10] In contrast, most of Clinton's supporters that were *actually there for the speech* did not seem to know what the alt-right was.[11] The alt-right, once again showing its nimble navigation in the political landscape, its control of the media, and its general awareness and ease of mobilization, got #AltrightMeans trending on Twitter, exposing even more people to their ideas in perfect timing for Clinton's speech.

The speech had complaints about Trump's racism and how he treats others, but she soon moved on to the alt-right, which she poorly explained. She tied Alex Jones to the alt-right; no connection. She said that Stephen Bannon and Breitbart were part of the alt-right; the mistake is forgivable since Bannon said that Breitbart was "the platform for the alt-right."[12] It is obviously not, but who knows what Bannon heard while talking to Yiannopoulos.

Hillary's anticipated speech devolved into a train wreck. When Clinton mentioned the Twitter user, @WhiteGenocideTM, even Rosie Gray was in disbelief.[13] Clinton then continued with discussing Nigel Farage, and went on to say that "the grand godfather of this global brand of extreme nationalism is Russian President,

Vladimir Putin." She tied Farage to Putin, Farage to Trump, and Trump to Putin. Anyone who knows anything about the alt-right or Farage would immediately laugh at this claim because of its absurdity (and how stupid Clinton sounded when she said all of this).[14,15] She next mentioned David Duke, but probably just to insert another scary name in her wild conspiracy.

This single speech from Hillary Clinton perhaps did more for the alt-right than any other event.[16] The alt-right had a few articles published about it and some references in the news, but it was all speculation or on the "fringe." Sam Dickson, a speaker in the alt-right, said, "I want you all to raise a glass and toast Hillary Clinton… Hillary Clinton did more for us than Donald Trump has done." He credited Clinton with pushing the alt-right ahead by about 30 years.[17] One of the cohosts of *Fash the Nation*, an alt-right podcast, later said that "…[Hillary] took out a giant, neon sign in Times Square to tell everybody about this new political movement… She's just growing the movement… I thought this was great for us."[18] It was.

Before this, essentially no one knew what the alt-right was except for a few journalists and some ultra-liberals who keep up with news relating to America's "racism." Even when it came to Republicans hearing about the alt-right, they just tried to push it under the rug or pretend it did not exist. The typical Republican does not think they are racist, but that *Democrats* are the real racists. They thought people voting for Trump had sincere concerns for the economy and immigration. They knew they and their friends were sincere, and that other Trump voters were too. Most average Republicans thought Clinton was directing her accusations of racism at *them* for supporting Trump. This assumption was confirmed fifteen days later when she said half of Trump's supporters fit in a "basket of deplorables."

It was not just that. Clinton said that some are "irredeemable" and "they are not America."[19] She further alienated already estranged people. Conservatives ignored the alt-right and liberals hoped it would go away, but all Clinton did was push more people into it. The alt-right will not be ignored and is not going away. Thanks, Hillary.

3

Risk of identifying as alt-right and early confusion.

The meaning of "alt-right" became more important when Donald Trump appointed Stephen Bannon to lead his campaign, and Hillary Clinton referenced Bannon about a week later in her speech. People were still wondering what the alt-right was and public figures began aligning themselves with the alt-right, believing that it was essentially anyone who supported Trump.

Lauren Southern tweeted a photo with the Danish flag and wrote "#AltRightMeans I don't have to be ashamed of my heritage."[1] This is comical because he[2] later tweeted out a video of him revealing his heritage/DNA test.[3] The video was set to private and the tweet was later deleted. Seems like he might not have been so proud of his heritage when he found out he was mainly western European with only 19% Danish (Scandinavian) and a 10% chunk of Spain.[4] To continue, he was called a white supremacist for that tweet[5] (things like that are driving mainstream men like Southern into the alt-right and it has been noted by Richard Spencer that "people are being pushed into the same boat").[6] Southern later explained that the alt-right was the "alternative right. People who are not establishment. Describes a lot of different groups - some of which I reject."[7]

Unfortunately, it is a bit more specific than that. Also unfortunately, Paul Nehlen, who ran (and lost) against Raul Ryan this current year, also used #AltrightMeans. He tweeted: "#AltRightMeans putting Americans first. The Alt-Right is an emerging force in politics engaged to #StopTPP and elect America 1st candidates."[8] He's right, but stopping the TPP is not one of the alt-right's priorities. It would be a strategic move for them, but if you search for a definition of the alt-right, "TPP" would not show up. While Nehlen is almost certainly not alt-right, he does retweet[9] them and loves Marine Le Pen,[10] the alt-right's French version of Trump. While the alt-right does not really have any candidate holding its views, it supports those like Trump and Le Pen.

Amidst the confusion there were two Internet celebrities who jumped into, out of, and back into the alt-right: Paul Joseph Watson and Mike Cernovich (neither are alt-right). Watson tweeted that he was in the alt-right,[11,12] then out of the alt-right.[13,14] In November 2016, Richard Spencer held a conference where some attendees did the Roman salute. The mainstream media was quick to use this as proof the alt-right was a white supremacist, Nazi movement. Watson tried to distance himself from the "tainted" term of "alt-right" by attempting to explain that there was the racist alt-right and the "new right."[15] Lana Lokteff, an alt-right media personality, was quick to note that "the New Right is straight from Europe" and that the title Watson chose was already in use.[16] Watson further distanced himself from Spencer by calling him a "clown"[17] and "white supremacist"[18] while writing that "[Spencer] has a tiny audience and the media suddenly made him king of the 'Alt-Right'. Incredibly suspicious."[19] Watson also said that it "Wouldn't surprise me if Richard B. Spencer is a fed..."[20] So to sum it up, Richard Spencer coins "alternative right" and uses the shortened label for years, and now Watson explains the mainstream media "loves"[21] "darling"[18] Spencer and has crowned him the "king"[19] of the alt-right in an attempt to disenfranchise the true alt-righters like Watson (while Watson doesn't consider himself alt-right anyway).

Mike Cernovich, an independent reporter, author and news breaker, claimed that he was alt-right.[22] He later deleted his statement and distanced himself by saying multiple times he was not alt-right,[23] while noting that the mainstream media calls him a "mastermind" of the altright,[24] and he suggested that Spencer was a federal agent to label Trump supporters as neo-Nazis.[25] After all this, Spencer wondered why Cernovich would denounce him when Ann Coulter, who is more mainstream, "is more of a badass... [Coulter] basically defended the conference [using] sarcastic comments."[26]

An alt-right Youtuber said Watson had "incredible dishonesty" during this confusion.[27] Another alt-righter criticized Watson, wondering why, if Spencer was a "plant," he would be banned from Twitter while Watson and Cernovich were not.[28] An alt-right activist thought it was ridiculous for people to be upset at the salutes.[29] Another alt-right Youtuber speculated that the alt-right movement might be dead since it was now associated with the toxic brand of Nazism.[30] Jared Taylor, who runs an alt-right organization, "...was very surprised [and] very saddened by it."[31]

Not only was there confusion about the alt-right to begin with, but Watson and Cernovich sent out all of this to their over half of a million followers (that's from Twitter alone). No wonder there is confusion when public figures claim they are alt-right, say it is not white supremacy, then say it is white supremacy, then say they are not alt-right, and then claim they are "New Right," which happens to be already associated with a European form of the alt-right. Then Ann Coulter, who isn't alt-right, "defends" the alt-right more than people who used to say they were alt-right. With this mass hysteria, one would say, "Please, just stop." But wait! There's more.

Cernovich joined Watson in an interview where they both criticized Richard Spencer, his conference, and the Nazi salutes at it. Cernovich was also there to explain to Watson's audience what Spencer's conference was about.[25] Henrik Palmgren and Lana Lokteff of Red Ice, an alt-right media platform, responded to those criticisms.[32] They asked why Watson did not invite Spencer on to discuss his conference since Cernovich was not even there.

Cernovich wondered why the conference only had a couple hundred people if it's so mainstream. To answer him, why would people show up to an alt-right conference if the alt-right is a movement stigmatized and called racist by leftists and right-wingers? The alt-right is bigger than Watson and Cernovich, but people cannot openly be alt-right. Alt-right Twitter user, @Ricky_Vaughn99, had thousands of followers and was rated the 107th highest election influencer by MIT, which was higher than @TheDemocrats and @NBCnews. Cernovich didn't make MIT's list and Vaughn's influence would be even higher if he had not been banned from Twitter.[33] Also, *Fash the Nation*, an alt-right podcast, was banned from Soundcloud after repeatedly having their episodes hit #1 in the political category. Alt-righters can't gain influence because they are banned once they start drawing attention. Additionally, Richard Spencer was banned from Twitter less than a week before his conference.[34] Coincidence?

If alt-righters are public with their views, they will get doxed, fired, attacked, or stalked:

> 1. Years ago, Carrie Bowe took part in a video featuring white women discussing race. She does not actually say anything

racist, but she is labeled a white supremacist and was fired from her job this year. She said that the video was edited and did not know what the end product would be and that she just wanted to start a conversation on race.[35]

2. Daily Record, while reporting on Millennial Woes, said that "Some anti-fascist campaigners have spent more than a year trying to identify [him]..." and at the end of the article they asked their readers to give them information on him if they had any.[36]

3. Riverfront Times published the personal information of a young, alt-lite[37] lady's family after she uploaded a video on Youtube talking about race and crime in St. Louis, MO.[38]

4. "A top editor at Politico quit over a social media post in which he suggested attacking white nationalist Richard Spencer — who happens to be his own neighbor." He also released Spencer's two addresses.[39]

5. Emily Youcis, after attending Spencer's conference to film and report on it, was fired from her job.[40,41]

6. More than one young person has claimed to be stalked by someone I won't name here.[42,43]

7. Sherry Spencer was demonized and threatened since her son is public with his views.[44]

So you see. The alt-right is more popular than Cernovich, but the alt-right keeps being attacked. Now back to Watson. Watson continued the interview with Cernovich by saying the media cuts and crops him to frame its narrative. Red Ice asks why Watson believes the media's frame of Spencer.

In response to the fact that National Socialists might actually be at Spencer's conference, Red Ice said that everyone knows the alt-right is a "big tent," so of course there might be a few there. Red Ice explained that during the conference, it's not surprising four people might do the Roman salute (Watson said "at least" 15) out of 350 people (who were drinking) over three days.

Red Ice explains that when right-wingers constantly are accused of being racists and Nazis by the left, the alt-right, being a humorful movement, throws those symbols and labels back in their face as a way of taking its power away and showing the left that they no longer care about being called names. "These labels are losing their [power]... We don't have to justify ourselves to these people..."

To clear up the confusion, it is safe to put Lauren Southern, Paul Nehlen,[45] Mike Cernovich, Paul Joseph Watson, Milo Yiannopoulos, and Ann Coulter into what the alt-right calls the "alt-lite," people who are essentially one step to the left of the alt-right. This confusion mounted up to so much that even Murdoch Murdoch, currently the most popular alt-right animators, did a dramatization of this conflict between the alt-right and the alt-lite.[46] Richard Spencer explained that, while he was being attacked by some of the alt-lite, he did not want to retaliate. He said, "There's also something to be said for not always punching directly to your left. Kind of allowing people [to] slowly evolve into your position... I've generally been more tolerant of these people, but I can't be tolerant of Cernovich when he's making accusations like this. It's just utterly ridiculous."[47]

Now the alt-right tried to avoid all this confusion, but perhaps not initially at the start. As noted above, Lana Lokteff of Red Ice said that the alt-right is a "big tent." Spencer also said that it was a "big tent" of right-wingers who were disillusioned by conservatives who supported George W Bush and the Iraq War while still calling themselves the "true conservatives." After observing their failings, Spencer said that they were "intellectually impoverished..." and the alt-right was "trying out a lot of different things. We were trying out the French New Right... the Ron Paul movement... anarcho-capitalism... Catholic traditionalism... The alt-right, in its [inception], was a kind of big tent... In a way, that was a very good thing."[48] Now maybe they wish they had set some rules before going public.

Perhaps Clinton's speech came too quick for them,[49] yet the alt-right *did* anticipated people listening to Hillary Clinton's speech and searching "What is the alt-right?" They made Youtube videos so people would get the right answer rather than get stuck in what ended up being a Yiannopoulos/Cernovich whirlpool. RamZPaul says in his video that the alt-right "...is about us [white people] having a home..." He says "...we don't want to hurt other people. We want to respect their right to self-determination, but we want our home. That's all it is. That's the alt-right."[50] Millennial Woes put up a video asking people if they liked the way things were going, and then listed alt-right people and websites for people to do more research.[51] Oscar Turner, a video designer, made a video compilation where Joe Biden says whites being a minority in America is good, Jared Taylor explains that celebrating diversity is "asking [whites] to celebrate their dwindling numbers," and Richard Spencer says that "We think race is biologically real... We have a passionate attachment to our extended family and the cultures and civilization that it birthed."[52]

Richard Spencer gave a monologue where he said, "Today, [whites] seem to have no idea who we are. We're rootless... We're often told that being an American, or a Briton, or German, or any European nationality, is about being dedicated to a collection of abstractions and buzzwords, 'democracy...' 'tolerance,' 'multiculturalism,' but a nation based on [this] is just another place to go shopping. It's a country for everyone, and thus a country for no one. It's a country in which we ourselves have become strangers... So long as we avoid and deny our

29

identities, at a time when every other people is asserting its own, we will have no chance to resist our dispossession. No chance to make our future. No chance to find another horizon. So who are we? I guess the real question is, 'Are we ready to become who we are?'"[53]

Jared Taylor put out a video saying that those in the alt-right have many viewpoints, "but they all agree one thing: equality is a dangerous myth... Races are different. They differ in average levels of intelligence. They do not build identical societies... Most people prefer the culture created by their own race and prefer to be around people like themselves. Blacks, Hispanics, and Asians express this preference all the time, and everyone thinks it's fine. It's only whites who are thought to be immoral if they openly prefer the culture, society, and people of Europe." He says that "The alt-right is eager to have the honest dialogue on race that former attorney general Eric Holder and others claim to want. Well, they're not sincere. They want to exclude everyone who disagrees with them. Honest dialogue is meaningless if everyone already agrees."[54]

4
What is the alt-right?

The alt-right is a white identity movement that focuses on ethnonationalism, which "is the idea that every distinct ethnic group should enjoy political sovereignty and an ethnically homogeneous homeland or homelands."[1] They believe ethnic groups have the right to maintain their majority in their country and not be reduced to a minority. This means Japan should stay Japanese, Germany German, and Nigeria Nigerian. Since the alt-right is a white movement, it acknowledges the right for others having "homelands," but it prioritizes whites. The alt-right began for all white Americans in general rather than specific ethnic groups because white Americans do not retain their original, specific group. Some critics may say that white nationalism does not make sense because different white ethnic groups fought against each other and do not have a common "white culture."[2] You can get around that rule if you consider

American whites an ethnicity, such as "American." It would be "American nationalism." That would make sense fifty years ago when American was synonymous with white, but since America has become more diverse, the term "white nationalism" is one that makes more sense.

Some on the alt-right, like RamZPaul and Jared Taylor, don't think America needs to be 100% white, but that it can be about 90% white and that would be acceptable for a white state. Most on the altright disagree with this.

The alt-right thinks that Japan has the right to be Japanese and no one tries to make them more diverse, so it is unfair that white countries must become more diverse. The reason they oppose diversity and immigration of non-whites is because they view it as a threat to white people and as a tool to eliminate them. White communities always "need" diversity and government policies have HUD bring in Section 8 housing to make areas more diverse, but black communities are not required to become more diverse.

Some of the reasons that the alt-right wants there to be a homeland for whites is so that they can practice their culture in peace, not be accused of racism for saying only "Merry Christmas" while not mentioning other holidays, or simply to be away from crime or not need to pay for welfare going to non-whites, which doesn't have an end in sight.

One may wonder why the alt-right thinks white people should get to have America, Canada, and Australia when they are not the natives. Most alt-righters would say that the Amerindians should get their own piece of North America to have an Amerindian ethnostate where they have total political power for their own country. Many alt-righters would say that black Americans can have a few states for themselves so white people can't discriminate against them anymore and they will be free from racism.

The alt-right views itself as motivated by love for their own, not hate for others. They despise the KKK and American Nazi Party because it tarnishes the alt-right's reputation if the alt-right is tied to them. While the KKK is known for lynching people and staging attacks on churches and schools, the alt-right tries to avoid hate, except when it makes a good joke. For instance, Walt Bismarck, an alt-right singer who makes song parodies, made one called "Fourteen Eighty Eight." 14 is a fourteen-word slogan, "We must secure the existence of our people and a future for white children." H is the eighth letter of the alphabet, so 88 means Heil Hitler. Bismarck said that he agrees with the 14, but not the 88, yet he still made the song simply because it made for a good song.[3] Even though the alt-right says it is not hate, they still do things like this because it is fun and humorous to them. Humor is an important factor in the alt-right and it is credited for getting the movement this far. Older identity movements did not make it anywhere because they failed attract people though humor and fun.[4] Ann Coulter said that "Now, having discovered these teenagers, they're really leading the way in taunting the media and the liberals. [Their position is:] 'Actually it is fun to be called a racist.'"[5,6]

The alt-right agrees with the right when it comes to valuing traditional roles, abstaining from non-traditional sex acts (homosexuality and open relationships), and its opposition to vices like drugs. They disagree with the left when it comes to transgenderism, diversity, excessive abortion, abstract and modern art, and its disdain for traditional America.

The alt-right agrees with the left when it comes to protecting the environment, organic/healthy foods/eating, protecting endangered animals and ecosystems, taxing things like sugary drinks, and caring for the poor. Many are vegans or follow the paleo diet. The alt-right disagrees with the right when it comes to excessive consumerism and interventionism. The alt-right views the fast-food, Black Friday spending culture to be a way for people to substitute possessions for relationships. The alt-right disagrees with the right's "Reagan worship" and "Constitution worship," and it dislikes the Church when it comes to giving money for foreign missions to the Third-World.

About 25% of the alt-right believes in socialism because it is important to take care of others in their race and about 25% believe in capitalism because free markets created the wealthiest countries, but the last 50% believe in a mixed economy that is about 80% capitalist and 20% socialist because they believe unfettered, capitalist individualism divides people as a race and there needs to be a little socialism to hold everyone together in a cohesive group that realizes they are family and need to take care of one another. This would make sense if you realize that some of the "socialist" Scandinavian countries have freer markets and lower taxes than America. They see that and go, "Hey, I guess socialism is kind of okay."

The alt-right disagrees with both parties when it comes to immigration. The Democrats want unlimited immigration and the Republicans want a lot of immigration. The alt-right, being nationalistic, supports Trump's "fair trade" and opposes trade deals and "free trade" that make it harder for the white, working class while benefiting foreigners. They oppose the European Union [EU] for not allowing individual countries to pursue their own interests. They oppose wars that have no benefit for themselves and they view them, and also the EU, as tools for the current mass migration of North Africans and Middle Easterners into Europe. Most all of the alt-right views Jews as the primary drivers of the white population decline, anti-white rhetoric and policies of the government and institutions, and mass migration, all culminating in the estimation of almost all white countries to have a white minority in the next eighty-five years (they actually will).[7] This is, at first glance, conspiratorial, but one must remember that blacks and Hispanics blame almost all of their misfortune on a "racist" white people, and, even though minorities are overrepresented as government employees[8] and there is a black president, Obama is just "a change of leadership for a mind-numbing apparatus of normalized repression and mass-based social violence..." and it "will not change." "...The figure of Obama represents a new inhabitation of white supremacy's structuring logics of violence."[9] One wonders, if not *knows*, that even if the President, Supreme Court, and both houses of Congress were 0% white (while still upholding current policies), that white people would still be considered privileged and the US government a system of oppression.

The alt-right is elitist when it comes to traditional fashion and it has an antipathy for modern style that is characterized by either SJWs or the stereotypical Wal-Mart shopper.

It views the Catholic Church as superior to Protestantism when it comes to architecture, and the culture that sometimes conflicts, like Catholic traditions opposed to the Prosperity Gospel. The alt-right is not a Christian movement, and it recognizes Christianity's cultural importance in uniting European peoples as one, but it also views Christianity as a feminized religion that is too weak when it comes to standing up for white people. Alt-righters frequently note that people incorrectly refer to the alt-right as a Christian movement.[10] There is quite a number of pagans, agnostics, and atheists in the alt-right. In spite of this Richard Spencer was happy to note that "Vladimir Putin wants to do some things that I think are very productive, such as promoting Russian identity and promoting the Orthodox Church."[11] This is for its cultural reasons in uniting a people and spreading traditional moral values and high culture, not for actually being Christian.

The alt-right wants a strong national defense and wants to bring back tough physical education in schools. They want a country that celebrates strength rather than weakness. This comes at a time during the 2016 Democratic National Convention when the spotlight shines on the disabled for all to see: Tom Harkin using sign language; Anastasia Somoza and Dynah Haubert in wheelchairs; a midget, Ryan Moore; blind Timmy Kelly; and a confused, apparently blind delegate leading one Pledge of Allegiance while a Paralympic, Mallory Weggemann, leads another. Writer, Ronnie Polaneczky, gushes how "Disability visibility is having a beautiful moment at this convention, and here's why: This is the most accessible convention the Democratic National Committee has ever produced. There are more ramps and wheelchair-seating areas this year..." Polaneczky also wrote that "400 delegates with disabilities are at the convention..."[12] In this current year the left glamorizes and celebrates the blind, the crippled, and the deformed. The alt-right celebrates beauty and strength.

5

Origin of the alt-right, its culture, and how it uses the Internet.

Internet culture is almost defined by the fact that people can anonymously participate in mostly every website or group. This naturally leads to people making rude comments, using racial slurs, and joking about taboo subjects like pedophilia. In the case of the latter, anonymity is no longer important since left-wing sites like Salon and Slate seem to be attempting to normalize it.[1,2] The alt-right is mainly a young [read: Internet using] generation who are further regulated to the Internet when discussing their views. This leads to the inevitable mashup of cultures. Imageboards (basically discussion forums plus images) like 4chan, /pol/ specifically (it's the political section of the site), become a hub for subjects that are not discussed in polite company. Anonymity fuels "trolling," which is joking with someone or making comments intended specifically to make them mad or upset, all while making them look like a fool. The alt-right is not entirely defined by jokes, memes, and trolling, like

41

Yiannopoulos says, but the fact that 4chan, Reddit, and 8chan were some of the best options for online discussion, alt-righters were pushed toward them and over the years the cultures have blended.

Pepe the frog is a meme that became popular as a reaction image, which some may post after reading what someone else wrote on the web. It is for conveying happiness, sadness, anger, etc. 2015 and 2016 were marked by the alt-righters developing Pepe into a Nazi and posting him in comments or replies to journalists, reporters, and anyone else who disliked or criticized Trump. Now the majority of those using Pepe use him as a simple reaction image, but since alt-righters on Twitter specifically used him to make reporters upset, they eventually started reporting on this happening. The momentum led to the alt-right "memeing"[3] the Anti-Defamation League [ADL] into classifying Pepe as a hate symbol.[4]

The alt-right's infatuation with Pepe eventually led to the creation of a satirical religion, where Pepe became the deity, Kek, through apotheosis. Kek is actually an Egyptian god that looks like a frog, and kek is a translation for lol (laugh out loud). So you can see how real life items, when just slightly resembling a part of the alt-right, become infused into the movement. The alt-right now says things like "Praise Kek."

Trolling was very important originally in order to grab the public's attention and create fun and humor that would attract young people. While speaking at an alt-right conference, F Roger Devlin dismissed trolling and encouraged the alt-right to drop the habit. "We need to raise our sights. We need to understand that the kind of people we may be tempted to troll are simply not worth our time..."[5]

Most of the current alt-right discussion and social matter happens on Twitter, led by people like Jared Taylor Swift and Paul Town, and an alt-liter, Jared Wyand, who is probably going to become alt-right due to their successful run of using (((echoes))).[6] An alt-right website, The Right Stuff, created a meme where Jewish names "echo." This became triple parentheses in written form and was used to identify Jews. This was memed into reality later in the 2016 election cycle after repeated use on Twitter to identify Jewish journalists led to it being used *by* them as a symbol of pride. This backfired by facilitating the harassment of Jews online. Following in the idea that

Jews are likely behind most anti-white policies, Jared Wyand noted that "The AltRight tricked Jews into putting ((())) around their names and I started noticing where all the anti-White propaganda comes from."[7] The ADL eventually ended up by labeling the echoes as a hate symbol.[8]

Twitter began banning alt-righters such as Wyand, Richard Spencer, Paul Town, @_Altright_ (now @_Altright_Anew), and Reinhard Wolff, along with alt-liters like Charles Johnson and Milo Yiannopoulos, and that led to the popularity of Gab, a Twitter alternative that allows its users to have free speech. Walt Bismarck, Jared T Swift, and Prince Hubris even set their accounts to private to avoid harassment or banning (you only get banned if people report you and they can only do that if they can see your tweets, hence setting your account to private).

When journalists report on the alt-right lexicon, the leftist ones say things like "The Racist Alt-Right Dictionary: 7 Terms You Need to Know…"[9] and the cuckservative[10] ones say "Deadly Words You Must Learn…"[11] If only the alt-right had its own lexicon pages on their sites so people knew what they meant. They do. Let's examine some of their lexicon.

A leftover relic from 4chan/Reddit culture is that the alt-right jokes about vaccines and autism and they joke about Barron Trump being autistic.[12] The more passionate about the alt-right you are, the more autistic you are. You can be a "wagecuck" (someone who sacrifices their life for money), or be an "autist" and eventually become an "autiste" who is "An Autistic person who has elevated their place on the spectrum to a work of art."[13] This comes from the stereotype of autistic people being very smart or a genius in their field or interest.[14] The most "autistic" alt-righters, autistes, are the ones who achieve making fashy memes on the Internet that get retweeted by Ann Coulter,[15] do not have jobs, or are "childless single men who masturbate to anime."[16,17]

The alt-right has achieved some things: Fascism is the most looked up word for Merriam Webster, which means it will be the Word of the Year.[18] The alt-right has made young men no longer rebel against society by doing drugs, but by getting "high on traditional moral values" because that is the ultimate act of rebellion in this current year.[19]

The alt-right also has its icons. 2013 was the year that the media picked up on a Pinterest user who took quotes from Adolf Hitler and put them on pleasant pictures of Taylor Swift.[20] The posts were all removed after being found out by the wider populace,[21] but the impact remained. Taylor Swift, a blue-eyed blonde who, for her age and social group, dressed classy and traditionally, became the type of pop figure for the alt-right during the 2016 election cycle. The media once again picked up on this during the summer of 2016. The alt-right projects their beliefs on remarkable public figures as a type of person to look up to in order to keep them going in their struggle. Sam Hyde, a comedian, did not get the nice treatment that Swift did. Whenever there is a shooting or other horrific event, the alt-right blames Hyde and posts pictures supposedly proving that he was the shooter. This has roots in 4chan and the alt-right engages in this also, doing it partially in order to troll the media and even succeeding more than once. [22] Forbes has a piece explaining much of this, and the author reached out for Hyde to comment on being framed for these crimes:

"My wife's boyfriend (open relationship) heard it from the news first and so he and my wife's son were both scared silly... I also got a call from my rabbi frantically trying to talk me out of doing anything more violent until finally I managed to explain..."[23]

There are even more icons that are raised as the alt-right's "leaders" in order to troll them. There was the celebrity chef, Guy Fieri;[13] trolls modifying images by the cartoonist, Ben Garrison, to make them appear anti-Semitic,[24] causing Garrison to eventually run with the caricature and make cartoons about Donald Trump and ending SJWs and political correctness; and now Steven Crowder, a conservative talk-show "make,"[25] became their latest figurehead,[26] and now even David Duke says that

"Hearing this guy, it may be a little bit extreme for me, but [I] really like him a lot, even though he's a lot more extreme [than me] in my Klan days... Even though he may be a bit extreme

47

for us, [we] have to give him... a helping hand and a big thanks for his courage in coming out for saving the white people of this country..."[27]

Considering you now know some of the cultural feel that the alt-right has, here are some ways you can identify someone who is alt-right in real life. Note: Many people have four or five of these traits but more than ten means you are most likely dealing with an alt-righter:

1.   He's a Millennial.
2.   Male.
3.   White.
4.   He wants an ancestry DNA test.
5.   He spends a lot of time reading or being on the Internet.
6.   He has a fashy haircut.[28]
7.   He loves Donald Trump.
8.   He used to like Milo Yiannopoulos.[29,30]
9.   He uses the word "cuck."
10.   He uses the signal word "limb" rather than "leg," even when referring to tables and chairs.[31]

11.   He sings about IQ tests,[32] or how "Love is a Giant Wall."[33]

12.   He uses the oven more often.

13.   He displays "prepper" behavior, like stocking food or weapons and worrying about WW3 or a civil war.

14.   He eats healthier and works out for said wars.

15.   He seems like he's becoming an exhibitionist and talks about how important beauty is.[34]

16.   He mentions border walls, Trump's Muslim ban, race crime stats, or is a Putin fan.[35]

17.   He likes traditional art or architecture.

18.   He wants many children.

19.   He not only dislikes liberals, but most Republicans too, even the "Constitutionalist Conservative" ones.

Things exclusive to females:

20.   Loves braids.

21.   Shuns makeup or only uses a little and natural colors.

22.   Wears modest dresses.

23.   Dances in wheat fields.

Hopefully you can use this guide to find the alt-righter in your life, but let's take a look at the actual alt-right Internet personalities and what they do.

6

Alt-right personalities and websites.

Alt-right coiner, Richard Spencer, runs the National Policy Institute, a white nationalist think tank. They occasionally publish research papers, but the most visible workings of the operation are podcasts, Radix Journal, a blog, and videos that Spencer often releases, and conferences held to discuss nationalism and help alt-righters to network. Big figures in the alt-right come to speak at the conferences and this gives alt-righters a chance to meet the thinkers who have an intellectual influence on them. In November there was a conference held and at the night-before dinner, ANTIFA protestors rushed the restaurant and obnoxiously yelled about fascism and white supremacy.[1] On December 6 (of course 2016) Spencer gave a speech[2] at Texas A&M which appeared to bring in his largest audience to date with 400 attendees.[3,4] With the rise of Donald Trump, Spencer has been getting many mentions on the mainstream television networks.

Jared Taylor runs American Renaissance, a platform discussing racial crime news and white advocacy. AmRen holds conferences and takes a slightly different view than the National Policy Institute (not discussing Jews too much). Taylor is a soft-spoken "white supremacist" who uses this so people will listen to him. He often talks about the hypocrisy of those who say that minorities can have pride and whites cannot, and he picks out almost any aspect of things minorities do that whites would be considered racist for doing.

Peter Brimelow runs VDARE, a website that is slightly milder than the typical alt-right sites, but it still hosts alt-right ideas and is mainstream enough to be retweeted and followed by Ann Coulter on Twitter. It primarily focuses on immigration (while ignoring most white nationalist or separatism terms) and is set up to appear as a reputable news site. If you send them an email asking about a topic, they will write a post on it, thoroughly explaining your question.[5]

Red Ice is a media group based in Sweden and the US. It is ran by Henrik Palmgren and Lana Lokteff (the background partners are Fredrik Tormann and Reinhard Wolff, with Emily Youcis maybe becoming an addition) and started off as a more conspiratorial type of website before evolving into a primarily pro-white news outlet. They livestream protests, conferences, and speeches, and have radio programs and news segments, such as "Cuck of the Week," which I think they might be slacking on. Since Red Ice does not have professional cameramen or easily portable equipment, the protests they livestream are typically filmed by alt-right volunteers who happen to be near the location of the protest, but Red Ice plans on expanding. They report anti-white violence and propaganda, but they also discuss milder things, like having a female guest on to discuss motherhood or feminism. They interview authors and activists in the alt-right movement.

The Right Stuff is a blog that publishes quite a few authors and puts out a couple of podcasts and it is geared toward the average guy. *Fash the Nation* is their most popular podcast, hosted by Jazzhands McFeels and Marcus Halberstram, which comes out every Saturday night (or Sunday morning if they're late). They discuss politics and their thoughts on what should be done in the movement while often having a guest on (typically a Twitter user). They are dying to get Ann Coulter on.

The Daily Stormer is a Republican news site that isn't alt-right, but it claimed to be the #1 alt-right website when the term became popular during the election. After Donald Trump won, Andrew Anglin, its editor, changed the header to "America's #1 Most-Trusted Republican News Source." As a Republican site, it publishes news from the point of view of the right, but it is different from the alt-right.

There are quite a few alt-right Youtubers and one of the oldest ones is RamZPaul, who regularly puts videos up where he discusses current events or makes satirical videos about them. He has given speeches at alt-right conferences and is like the nerdy, racist uncle you probably don't have.

Millennial Woes is a Millennial Youtuber who puts up videos on his deep thoughts about the alt-right and how they will gain their goals. He is Scottish and recently took a tour through America while staying at houses of his fans. He smokes in probably every video and he's fat, two things that his viewers constantly criticize him for.

Murdoch Murdoch is the most popular animator on the alt-right, frequently focusing on the three cartoon representations of the makers of the videos in their fictional, alt-right universe. Watch out for Emily Youcis.[6] Timothy Murdock does a podcast and makes cartoons that are extremely popular. He made a video entitled, "How Whites Took Over America," in which he portrayed whites as simply bringing diversity to America and he explained the importance of race.[7] He also made the cartoon, "AntiRacist Hitler," where Hitler comes back and pushes for diversity in Israel, leading to the genocide of the Jews.[8] I should add that Walt Bismarck makes alt-right parodies of Disney songs and Oscar Turner posts videos with usually inspirational monologues.

Evalion, her real name was exposed as Veronica Bouchard, is a Canadian Millennial who made videos supporting Donald Trump and the alt-right. After being influenced by Sinead McCarthy (a more extreme activist who thinks the earth is flat), Evalion became a critic of Trump as being just a tool. She gained many followers when LeafyIsHere (famous Youtuber) made a video about her. Onision, an SJW Youtuber, sent his subscribers to report Evalion for hate speech, leading her channel to be taken down and further radicalizing her by reinforcing her beliefs that pro-white people *will* be banned from online platforms. Evalion asked for donations while she began making an audiobook of Mein Kampf, but she never followed through because "I just couldn't get the sound right."[9]

On Twitter there are hordes of alt-righters, but here are some notable ones. @_Altright_Anew has taken up the cause of alt-right networking. He pairs people up in states and encourages others to meet up and build friendships with like-minded people. @TheeCurrentYear is an investigative reporter[10] for the alt-right, frequently bringing you everything you need to know about the current "happenings," meaning that he finds videos, photos, and articles on the web of either alt-right conferences, events, or protests, or riots or protests by Black Lives Matter and others. @Third_Position regularly shares pictures and graphics showing differences between whites and non-whites, and spends time spreading alt-right views to many individuals each day and pointing out supposed hypocrisy that whites face.

There are definitely authors that make up the intellectual backbone of the alt-right and there are multiple books alt-righters can buy, but since the alt-right is a younger movement concentrated mainly on the Internet, many alt-righters may not even know who these intellectuals are and today's young people *are* known for disliking reading. Another reason this "generation gap" is amplified is because, with many alt-righters trying to maintain anonymity, they will refrain from making purchases that can be tracked back to them, and these books and materials do actually cost money, something that a few people are short on nowadays.

Now that we have gone through what the alt-right is, its history, and the people making it up, let us examine what drives someone into the alt-right.

"**Article II**

In the present Convention, genocide means any of the following acts committed with intent to destroy, in whole or in part, a national, ethnical, racial or religious group, as such:

(a) Killing members of the group;

(b) Causing serious bodily or mental harm to members of the group;

(c) Deliberately inflicting on the group conditions of life calculated to bring about its physical destruction in whole or in part;

(d) Imposing measures intended to prevent births within the group;

(e) Forcibly transferring children of the group to another group."[11]

United Nations Convention on the Prevention and Punishment of the Crime of Genocide

7

How do people become alt-right?

The alt-right has what it calls "red pills," which are facts, figures, thoughts, or opinions that, when taken (accepted as fact) by people, they become more alt-right. The red pill has its origin and evolution,[1] but the alt-right has picked it up and is currently its most vocal user. If you have been "red pilled," that means you became alt-right. If you were "red pilled" on a certain topic, that means you accepted that specific thing as fact. Richard Spencer even put up a section of his site named "The Red Pill" with articles intended on converting people to the alt-right.[2] Alt-righters frequently ask others what their "red pill experience" was like and *Fash the Nation* even had a collection of audio clips from their podcast focusing on it.

Let's start off with defining "white countries," being all European countries, Russia, Australia, Canada, and America. This is where a leftist would say countries like America, Canada, and Australia have never been

100% white and were stolen by whites, but the alt-right, as earlier mentioned, would point out "hypocrisy" because other countries were "stolen," but only whites must feel guilty, and no one would say China is not an Asian country or a Chinese country, even though China has never been 100% Han Chinese (and has a history of taking over other places, such as Tibet). Alt-righters would ask why leftists say America is a white supremacist country, but not a "white country." Also, alt-righters would say that saying America is a "nation of immigrants" means nothing because every nation is a "nation of immigrants," and that no leftist would say America is a Christian country, even though there are more Christians than immigrants. So, to simplify this explanation on why people become alt-right, let's not get hung up on semantics because I just used an entire paragraph getting derailed from the point, which is red pills (facts) that convert people to the alt-right.

Demographic transformation is one of the main reasons an average white person becomes an alt-righter. It is surprisingly difficult to find racial demographics of the world, but, by year, it is roughly estimated that in 1950, white people were 27% of the total population, in 2010 they were 13%, and in 2050 they are estimated to be 8%. One can search each individual country and add them up, but it is quite time consuming, especially when you must factor in demographics of each country.

In addition to those figures, white people in white countries are all currently not having enough children to replace themselves. "In 2014, the total fertility rate in the EU-28 [European Union countries] was 1.58 live births per woman."[3] The total fertility rate (TFR) must be is 2.1 children born per woman in order to keep the nation's population the same with no increase or decrease. This is one child to replace the man, one to replace the woman, and .1 to make up for infant death or natural sterility in some humans. Alt-righters might display a list of the TFR of white countries to show people that white adults are not having enough children to replace themselves as they die. Here are such 2016 statistics from the CIA's World Factbook:[4]

United States, 1.87 [Note: This is an average TFR for all races in America. The white one is lower than this.]

Netherlands, 1.78

Australia, 1.77

Russia, 1.61

Canada, 1.60

Germany, 1.44

Slovenia, 1.35

Poland, 1.34

Now there are "non-white countries" that also are facing this problem, but alt-righters brush this off because they are not expected to let in millions of immigrants each year for diversity:

Iran, 1.83

Vietnam, 1.82

Lebanon, 1.73

Thailand, 1.51

Korea, South, 1.25

Next an alt-righter would say to look at non-white countries and see how high their TFR. Note: The highest TFR for a white country is 2.07, for France, taking 108th place out of the whole world. The 107 top countries for TFR are all non-white. Here are just the top 10:

1. Niger, 6.62

2. Burundi, 6.04

3. Mali, 5.95

4. Somalia, 5.89

5. Uganda, 5.80

6. Burkina Faso, 5.79

7. Zambia, 5.67

8. Malawi, 5.54

9. Angola, 5.31

10. Afghanistan, 5.22

After viewing the CIA's World Factbook, you can see how someone might be a little shocked at these numbers (in non-white countries) because a TFR of 6 means each generation is triple the previous one, and (in white countries) a TFR of 1.5 means each generation is ¾ of the previous one. Add to this poverty, the migrant crisis in Europe, and thousands of Central American immigrants coming into America illegally each year, and alt-righters would be wondering if it's so bad now that Central Americans must come to America and migrants to Europe, then what will it be like when these countries are triple their population in 30-40 years.

If you're still around after an alt-righter is explaining this to you through the Internet, they'll then move on to current demographics of white countries and their future racial projections, sharing headlines like these:

1. "Projections released by the U.S. Census Bureau show that whites will become a 'minority' by 2044."[5] This number includes North Africans and Middle Easterners as white, so the more appropriate year would be 2037, which is in 20 years.

2. "White children to become minority by 2020."[6] This also includes NAs and MEs as white, so whites are probably already a minority of children in the US.

3. "White Britons 'will be minority' by 2066."[7]

4. "Muhammed really is most popular baby name in the UK."[8]

5. "8 Percent Of US Newborns Are Anchor Babies."[9] That's 1/3 of total Hispanic births in the US.[10]

The alt-righter might then tell you that once whites become a minority, it doesn't magically stop. It speeds up.[11] You can dismiss this and tell an alt-righter that skin color doesn't matter and that diversity is a strength, but they will flip it around and ask, "What if white people were doing this to blacks and Hispanics? Turning Mexico white and Africa white." You might not choose your words carefully and come back with, "White people already did that: *colonization*, and they're getting back what they deserve." This opens up the conversation for the alt-righter to ask, "I thought diversity was a strength, and now you're saying it's punishment?" As I have written earlier, alt-righters always flip things around and try to pick out little contradictions that you might make.

While witnessing an Internet user debating with an alt-righter, it seems curious to me that when the opponent says race doesn't matter while discussing whites becoming a minority in some countries, the alt-righters never mention black cities in America not wanting to be white. It's a simple factoid the alt-right could weaponize, but they do not. For example, after population loss in Hurricane Katrina in 2006, the mayor,

Ray Nagin, said "I don't care what people are saying uptown or wherever they are. This city will be chocolate at the end of the day. [Applause.] This city will be a majority African-American city. It's the way God wants it to be. You can't have New Orleans no other way. It wouldn't be New Orleans."[12] I've never heard the alt-right reference this, but if they did it would probably go something like, "Why can't whites say, 'America will be white at the end of the day. America will be a majority white country. It's the way God wants it to be. You can't have America no other way. It wouldn't be America'? Oh, and if blacks should get New Orleans, what about the Native Americans?"

In another instance, Washington, DC, which was majority black, started having a population shift and blacks became the minority. An article from Slate had the title tag, "The plan is real. There is a plan to eradicate DC's black majority."[13] Another title was "For Ivy City, 'The Plan' isn't paranoia."[14] One wonders why an alt-right doesn't ask, "You get mad if two cities switch majorities, but we can't get mad if every white country does?" Even years later, people are still saying "Gentrification is the new colonialism."[15] An alt-righter would ask, "But is *immigration* colonialism?"

One example of what an alt-righter would say if someone says race does not matter or that America should have "radical inclusion" is ask if Israel should have radical inclusion. That's exactly what happened at Texas A&M when a rabbi explained why he thought Richard Spencer was wrong. The rabbi said, "You come here with a message of radical exclusion. My tradition teaches a message of radical inclusion and love…"[16] Spencer responded with, "Do you really want radical inclusion into the state of Israel…? Maybe all of the Middle East can move in… Would you really want that? [Pause] You're not answering." "I'm not answering," the rabbi affirmed. Spencer then said,

"The Jewish people… Why are they a people? They are a people *precisely* because they did not engage in radical inclusion. Jews exist *precisely* because you did not assimilate to the Gentiles… That is why Jews are a coherent people with a history and a culture and a future. It's because you had a sense of yourselves. I respect

69

that about you. I want my people to have that same sense of themselves. I want my people to survive in the future."[17]

Usually alt-righters avoid talking about Israel while trying to convince people because observers already have the "Nazi image" in their minds, but Spencer mentioned Israel since it was a rabbi asking the question. *Forward* later had a headline, "Speechless Rabbi Admits Losing Argument Over Racism and Israel..." and it was reported that the rabbi explained, "I wasn't on the high school debate team... I really didn't want to get into it."[18] This begs the question as to why the rabbi did not give an answer to *Forward*. I'm pretty sure he had time to think of one.

To continue on, it is inevitable in a debate with an alt-righter that they will bring up crime rates, such as blacks being thirteen times more likely to murder whites than the reverse.[19] They are sure to also say, "Imagine how bad the crime will be once whites are a minority." One statistic they never forget to mention is that 100% of American, interracial rapes between blacks and whites are black *on* white.[20] This is extremely misleading because there are *some* white-on-black rapes, but the number isn't high enough to register as a percent, so it's not actually 100%.[21]

Alt-righters like Paul Town compare crime rate and income level by putting up blogposts entitled, "The Richest Black Neighborhood In America Has A Higher Rate Of Crime Than The Poorest White Neighborhood In America,"[22] or @Third_Position putting up images comparing "Beattyville, KY, Poorest White area in the USA, Median Income: $14,871, Violent crime/100k ppl: 158," with "View Park-Windsor Hills, CA, Richest Black area in the USA, Median Income: $159,168, Violent crime/100k ppl: 196."[23] They repeat these numbers so much that they get upset when you ask for sources, so you spend an hour yourself searching to find out if they are true.

An alt-righter will almost always mention IQ differences between races and they point out they cannot be "white supremacists" if they think Asians are smarter. As for blacks being less intelligent, the typical response is a conservative saying the cause is "Educational and cultural values," or a liberals saying it's racism or discrimination. In response to that, alt-righters put up graphs[24] saying that children of rich blacks get *lower* SAT scores than children of poor whites.

Of course, this leads to the discussion on evolution and races being different. They begin with small things, like white people being more likely to get skin cancer and blacks being more likely to be vitamin D deficient, and then move on to bigger things, like testosterone difference (causing crime differences), time preference[25] differences (causing poverty and financial mismanagement), telling someone's race by bacteria in mouths, and whites being part Neanderthal and Asians being part Denisovan. They ask things like, "African and Asian elephants are completely unique and different species, but African and Asian humans are not?" or "African and European bees are different, but the people aren't?" Debate tactics, like discussing crime rates, IQ scores, the TFR, or evolution, differ depending on what they think will be easier to convince you. If noticing from your profile picture that you like dogs, they'll write something like, "So breeding dogs for 100 years makes a Great Dane different from a Chihuahua. They're both dogs, but no one would say they're equal, yet humans evolving separately for 50,000 years means *only* skin color is changed?"

One may wonder why different races actually existing or being different is important for alt-righters to point out. This is to further their idea that if races are different, they have the right to exist without interference from others and they have rights to their culture, way of life, and self-determination. Even though this is important, Jared Taylor explained that

"Even... on aesthetic grounds alone... I think we'd be justified in saying 'Well, gosh, I like the way white people look.' ...We take an interest in the appearance in our animals, our horses, our dogs. We care about the breed[s] of Labradors and pugs. I think that white people, Europeans, have a distinctive aesthetic that I think is admirable. I find them particularly pleasing, and even if someone doesn't, I think those differences, simply because they exist, are worth preserving. We care about these obscure species... There is a Cuban crocodile that is very similar to the American crocodile. Well, they're interbreeding and the Cuban crocodile [genes are disappearing.] Well, this is of great concern to biologists. They're trying very hard to think of ways to protect the gene pool of the Cuban crocodile. But white people for heaven's sake? Us? No. Who cares?"[26]

One example of an event that made more white people alt-righters is the Trayvon Martin shooting.[27] After knowing Martin had THC in his system while witnesses said he attacked George Zimmerman, and then the media called Zimmerman "white," and Barack Obama "called" Martin his son, then Zimmerman being harassed afterword and whites being attacked by blacks saying, "This is for Trayvon," many whites saw what they viewed as anti-white rhetoric and events, causing them to become alt-right. These conversions continued with the 2014 Ferguson unrest, 2015 Baltimore riot, 2016 San Jose attacks on Trump supporters, and 2016 Charlotte riot, proving once again that liberals and blacks convert more people to the alt-right than "racist," white conservatives do.

After saying all of this, there is still a question someone may ask. "Why should whites continue to exist? Why does it matter?" The alt-righter will flip it around with the response, "Why should blacks continue to exist? Why does it matter? Does saying it that way sound racist?" Imagine Richard Spencer asking, "Why should Jews exist?" Would that be okay, or can you only ask that about whites? It was apparently okay when Tim Wise, an opponent of the alt-right, wrote this of white right-wingers: "You're on the endangered list. And unlike, say, the bald eagle or some exotic species of muskrat, you are not worth saving."[28]

This brings us to statements by public figures and other instances when someone just watching television one night might see or hear something and become alt-right. Let's start with Black Lives Matter rushing the stage and taking it from Bernie Sanders (great video, must watch).[29] Speaking of Bernie, he is a Democrat running for president in 2016 who said during a debate, "When you're white, you don't know what it's like... to be poor."[30] Another instance this election was when a black, Democrat woman onstage said, "I need all white people to move to the back."[31]

Maybe white people go alt-right when just in the past month there was a lawyer who wanted to "automatically [acquit] African-Americans accused of murdering or raping whites, no matter what the facts."[32] Maybe it's because CNN broadcasts Symone Sanders, an African-American Democrat who says "We don't need white people leading the Democratic Party right now."[33] Maybe she's talking about wanting Keith Ellison to lead it. Ellison became the *frontrunner* for the chairman of the DNC after the election, in spite of, while discussing reparations for slavery, suggesting that

> "Blacks would have the option of choosing their own land base or remaining in the United States. Since black people toiled most diligently in the southeastern section of the United States, this land, quite naturally, would be most suitable. That means Arkansas, Alabama, Georgia, Louisiana and Mississippi. Blacks, of course, would not be compelled to move to the black state, and, of course, peaceful whites would not be compelled to move away."[34]

That sounds pretty close to what Richard Spencer wants for whites, so why isn't Spencer being considered for chairman of the RNC? No members of the Congressional Black Caucus disavowed Ellison or his comments.[35] The only political appointee who is being criticized for racism is Steve Bannon. Even Anderson Cooper defended Bannon when Elizabeth Warren randomly attacked him as a "white supremacist."[36]

Maybe people are becoming alt-right because even when a black cop shoots a black man, the end result is blacks rioting and saying, "All white people are fucking devils."[37] Maybe white Americans become alt-right when they see:

1. Blacks kill whites at an extraordinarily high rate compared to whites killing blacks.
2. Blacks riot and blame whites for things other blacks did.
3. White people will soon be a minority, thus amplifying 1. and 2. (Don't forget, the decrease in the white population share then speeds up.)

Maybe whites become alt-right when Oprah Winfrey says, "There's still generations of people, older people, who are born and bred and marinated in it, in that prejudice and racism, and they just have to die."[38] Since many liberals think *all* white people are racist[39] and minorities *can't* be racist,[40] does that mean all whites "just have to die"?

Maybe whites become alt-right when tax payer, federally funded corporations call for job applications from people who are "Any race except Caucasian."[41] Maybe it's when that same corporation makes a music video saying, "Beige power, beige power… gonna look the same by the year 3000," and "Jump off the bland wagon and feel the beige power."[42] Is it serious, or just satirically calling for genocide? You decide. Red Ice responded to the video, asking, "It's okay to have beige power?" and "Look the same by the year 3000? So then that's not diversity?"[43] Also, the music video had 63 times as many dislikes as likes.

Maybe whites become alt-right when they hear what Google says is a problem, and then see what they do to fix it. Google released their workforce diversity statistics of 2014, which show whites (61%), Hispanics

(3%), and blacks (2%) *under*represented and Asians (30%) *over*represented. Whites are 65% of the US population, hence underrepresented at Google, and Asians are 5% of the US population, hence overrepresented by 600%. Google released the statement on these statistics. "Google is not where we want to be when it comes to diversity, and it's hard to address these kinds of challenges if you're not prepared to discuss them openly, and with the facts." The statement later said, "But we're the first to admit that Google is miles from where we want to be—and that being totally clear about the extent of the problem is a really important part of the solution."[44] An alt-righter would look at that and ask, "Whites are underrepresented and you *still* say there isn't enough diversity? Are you anti-white?" A logical person would think Google may answer with something like, "Actually, we are going to increase the black and Hispanic *and* white shares of the workforce by lowering the share of Asians." That would make sense because Asians are the only ones overrepresented, but did Google do this, or, as alt-righters say, does diversity always mean "less white people"?[45] Let's skip forward and see how Google "fixed" their diversity problem. Google boasted, "We moved in the right direction. We're still not where we want to be when it comes to diversity, but last year, we made progress in our efforts to build a more diverse Google." So now let's compare 2014 to 2016.

2014: White 61%, Hispanic 3%, Black 2%, Asian 30%.
2016: White 59%, Hispanic 3%, Black 2%, Asian 32%.[46,47]

Literally all they did was subtract two points from whites, who are already underrepresented, and give them to Asians, who were already overrepresented and are now 640% overrepresented, yet Google celebrated this?

Now you can be a conservative and look at all of this and think, *Race doesn't exist. It's just culture and racism that makes these problems and we can fix all of this, after all, Hispanics are natural conservatives.* You become an alt-righter when you see this and think, *Let's just separate. We've been trying to get along for over 50 years and I don't want my descendants to live in a country for the next 200+ years as a hated minority where whites are more likely to be victims of interracial violence, liberals constantly whine about white privilege, and whites are underrepresented and it's still not enough "diversity."*

So, now that we've looked at reasons why people become alt-right, let's take a look at where it is going.

8

The future of the alt-right and living with it.

The alt-right seems to be a temporary movement, perhaps going from 2008-2028. Many in the alt-right explain why they think the alt-right title is only going to be useful for a while, and some think it is probably already headed out because of the four Nazi salutes at Richard Spencer's conference. An article was written explaining that "The Alt Right jokes about eugenics, genocide, sodomy, molestation, murder, nuclear weapons and slavery because we need to widen the window of discussion generally, not just the Overton window."[1] The writer explains how the alt-right was a tool that intentionally created controversy to get people discussing these topics, which would hopefully result in these becoming desensitized. The Overton window is the collection of topics that are publicly debatable and discussable while anything outside the window cannot be discussed. The alt-right was for bringing undiscussable topics into not necessarily the mainstream discourse, but the acceptable discourse.

Matt Lewis, commentator at CNN, explained that the alt-right's first goal is "actually to make white people... start being race conscious. That's the first strategy here, and they say things like, 'Look, why is it that other groups of people can take care of their own, and white people don't?' That's the first step here."[2] So what is the future of the alt-right?

As the alt-right disappears or progresses, there is a chance that it takes over the Republican Party. Richard Spencer even noted that "there's been a kind of 'alt-rightification' of mainstream conservatism."[3] He has also been saying lately (perhaps joking) that he may run for office in Montana.[4] Although the media says that Steve Bannon's appointment was tying the alt-right to the Republican Party, it was obviously not, and it will take much more time for the Republicans to become the alt-right if that were to happen. Some think it will and explain that "As the only intellectual perspective that can put together a coherent, scientifically based populist world view, [the alt-right] will thrive in the post-neocon/cuckservative political landscape."[5]

Ben Shapiro also wrote that "If Republicans aren't careful, they'll soon see true conservatism banished from their party."[6] This is utterly ridiculous. The alt-right can't ban something from the Republican Party if it's not there. Sure there are conservatives in the party, but that doesn't mean it's "conservative" any more than alt-righters being there makes it alt-right. You can't really call the party conservative when they cannot even conserve bathrooms (not to mention failing on abortion, immigration, trade, gay marriage, marijuana, etc.). That's why Trump and the alt-right are here. The Republican Party won't do anything, and the alt-right views itself as more conservative anyway.

There has been a suggestion by alt-righters to infiltrate Republican groups. An alt-righter gave a speech where he said he "would like to see a takeover of the... young Republicans on college campus... The people that are leading these groups [are sometimes alt-right already]." Another thought he had was "Perhaps eventually we'll start, like a white student's union... but actually [a better idea is] taking over the GOP groups and making the Republican Party an explicitly pro-white group." Later he said that "We should be infiltrating these groups. We should be taking them over, and then we should be converting as many people as possible in them, and then we should be using the money that these groups get... to invite our own speakers."[7]

If the alt-right doesn't take over the Republican Party, there are still many ways it can spread. After mass bans of alt-righters on Twitter, many decided to move to the "free speech version of Twitter," Gab, but others are fighting back. There is now a campaign (by some of the extreme alt-righters) to make fake, black Twitter accounts that are to be used for sowing discord in the black Twittersphere.[8] They are also using them for reporting people and getting them banned from Twitter, all as payback for Twitter banning alt-righters.

More mature alt-righters seek to network and put up flyers and signs promoting white identity. Alt-righters in Michigan are putting up posters to spread their identitarian views and even giving "interviews" on the Internet to other alt-righters to explain how to engage in activism.[9] They are quite knowledgeable about these topics and discuss things like custom tailoring materials to appeal to Christians (such as naming Islam and targeting Dispensationalism).

Putting up mild, non-racist material that later makes news for being a "racist" is also a goal. For example, American Vanguard put up posters of white people at the University of Central Florida with the phrases, "Free yourself from cultural Marxism," and "We have a right to exist." They later made the news and here are some quotes of the "in-depth" analysis of the posters:

1. "The posters have students and authorities on edge."
2. "The messages are hard to forget."
3. "They were very disturbing images."
4. "They use these images to... create a sense of fear and let people know there's a sense of hatred in this community."[10]

Besides anonymous activism, Identity Evropa actually held a demonstration in October 2016 against sanctuary cities at Pier 14 in San Francisco, where Kate Steinle was murdered. They collaborated with Red Ice to mislead protestors into thinking the gathering was at Malcolm X Plaza at San Francisco State University, a twenty-four minute drive away. There were protestors at the wrong location and even a news helicopter went out to film the event.[11]

Now when the alt-right moves from anonymous Internet activism and putting up posters secretly to actually interacting with people and spreading their message through in-person conversation, looks are important. Matt Tait, a British nationalist, gave a speech at a 2015 conference on the mistakes of the nationalist movement in the UK. He explained that

> "It's often been said that people's impression of you is 70% how you look, 20% how you speak, and 10% what you say... If we want to have people who can survive in these high pressure, high tension positions, we need to make sure [they] look good, and that they speak well, and really, details of policy... is something that isn't particularly crucial. Most of the time when I was involved in politics, the debates would be about 'Should we be in favor of this? Should we be against that? How much should we be against that? How should we define it?' Constantly trying to get that 10% of the important elements right,

and not focusing enough on the 70% or the 20%. Our message *is* our messenger. I'm gonna say that again because I think this is absolutely crucial. Our message *is* our messenger."[12]

So the alt-right is trying to spread their message with good-looking, presentable people, and it looks like they're succeeding.[13] Still, what happens if they succeed in gaining widespread support? If they want a white country, does that mean genocide, mass murder, mass deportations, and bloodshed? They actually discuss how they will get things done and some even have troubles accepting it.

Alt-righters point to historical instance of deportation, such as forcing millions of innocent Germans living in parts of Europe that were not Germany to move to Germany simply because of ethnicity. If the US can do that, then of course a "noble" goal of saving whites can have something similar. Then there are states like New Hampshire, Vermont, and Maine which are over 95% white. Considering the average American moves every 7 years,[14] the alt-right views financial incentives or job offers as likely ways to encourage non-whites to move.

Some alt-righters want more than just New Hampshire, Vermont, and Maine, but if you include a few more states, many alt-righters will settle for that rather than overtaking the whole United States.

Even those who do want the US to be white, violence and deportation (of non-white citizens) are not necessarily necessary. Donald Trump has already suggested banning Muslims and *all* immigrants until proper screening. At CPAC 2013 Trump also mentioned accepting mainly European immigrants.[15] In August, 2016, Joy Reid criticized Trump's immigration plans, writing that the "Idea of a commission to select 'desirable' immigrants 'with a high likelihood of success' is straight up alt-right push for Europeans only."[16] Also, the alt-right has celebrated Trump's childcare plan as a way to increase the white TFR while not increasing the TFR of the other races because it appears to primarily benefit whites. So there are just four examples that, if instituted, would make America whiter without violence (and without the alt-right even being in power). Additionally, after Trump won the election, #Calexit began trending on Twitter in support of California seceding from the US. That would also make America a whiter place and less leftist, perhaps guaranteeing a Republican president for the next thirty years.

Even RamZPaul and Jared Taylor, people spearheading the movement, have said they are okay with a roughly 90% white country. It's also important to note that the alt-right is the only significant American political movement that supports an independent country for Amerindians.

Now, there is the belief that violence will break out in the US or perhaps a race war may begin. The alt-right points out that there are ethnic conflicts in Europe and they also see the annexation of Crimea as another example of animosity between whites, so they wonder why America, a multiracial country, would not also experience these conflicts when the going gets tough. An alt-right Youtuber supposedly put up a video saying something like, "I'm leaving the alt-right because I cannot support violence." I write "supposedly" because the video is gone. There was a response video done by Millennial Woes directed at the Youtuber where he explained why violence was inevitable.[17] He told the Youtuber that the only way racial conflict can end peacefully is if whites give up their countries, "But even then, the fate of the last whites in Europe would be a very grim and violent one, so even then violence wouldn't be avoided." If someone thinks whites being a small minority would not result in their persecution, an alt-righter would point them to South Africa's dwindling white population and Haiti, where blacks wiped out the whites, and then even wiped out the blacks who were part white.

When you watch them for a few years and see what they discuss, you also see that they struggle with the fact that bad things might happen. I think this is one of the main factors that differentiates the alt-right from neo-Nazis and white supremacists. They actually care about discussing hard choices, which they actually view as hard, and trying to find the best possible outcomes. The fact that the Youtuber later deleted many videos, including that one, shows the doubt that many alt-righters have when it comes to violence (but, in their eyes, deporting non-white Americans is still morally superior to wiping out white Americans). Millennial Woes later set his video to private, furthering the fact that discussing and committing violence is not what the alt-right wants. The Youtuber made another video responding to Millennial Woes, and then later set the video to unlisted so that no one would find it. That's yet a third instance where alt-righters put material on the Internet saying they do not want violence, but *still* hide the videos from the public because they do not want to appear hateful.

Is the alt-right evil if it can live with violence that might come about during its attempt at getting a white ethnostate? An alt-righter would say that so many whites are raped and killed by non-whites that deportations are morally superior to knowingly allowing more crime to continue. I think the fact that they write articles like this[18] is proof that the alt-right is not maliciously evil (maybe just cautious to such an extent, or a liberal might think misled, that they are driven to the "solutions" that they now hold). Greg Johnson explains that people who agree with the alt-right still hesitate when it comes to making a white ethnostate because of the fear of being evil. Johnson writes that there are four questions to ask concerning the hard choices that might need to be made.

1. Is deporting people possible? Johnson writes, "Was it possible for them to come here? ...Most non-whites are moving anyway. We

just want their next move to be outside of our homelands."

2. When it comes to living with it, Johnson tries to justify his position by listing many ways people are forced to move and explaining that "White people seem to sleep quite well at night knowing that millions of people are forced to move for economic reasons, which all basically boil down to private greed." Johnson also mentions millions of whites being forced to move out of cities ruined by integration or immigration and says, "Whites are already living with ethnic cleansing [as] victims rather than the beneficiaries." Johnson later writes that one should not ask if whites can live with it, but if they can live without it.

3. As for the morality of it, Johnson writes that *if* whites are to become extinct, then "Ethnic cleansing... is simply a matter of self-defense..."

4. On it being icky (read: killing people), Johnson says, while permissible in self-defense, killing

is not necessary "and may even be counter-productive."

Johnson concludes his article with this:

"Many whites are uncomfortable about resettling non-whites who have put down 'roots' in our homelands. Non-whites have tens of thousands of years of roots in their homelands. Yet somehow they managed to move here... Most whites accept limits on our freedom to save endangered species of animals and plants... It is time to take the preservation of our own race just as seriously."

So the short-term future of the alt-right might be infiltrating Republican groups or spreading their message, and the long-term future might involve violence. The occurrence of violence is not an unreasonable happening considering ethnic conflicts in literally the whole world and race riots in America. Simply because we live in 2016 does not make us exempt from human history. The last question is: How can the alt-right be stopped?

9

How to end the alt-right.

The first thing a leftist thinks when they see something like the alt-right is *How do I kill it?* That's one "solution." A conservative ignores the alt-right and hopes it goes away. (Hint: It won't.) Both sides will say that during economic downturn, minorities are the scapegoat, and whites should just get jobs and things will settle down. That isn't going to work because the alt-right is already making waves. You might ban them from the Internet, but this won't work since they always bounce back. Even Richard Spencer's Twitter account was un-suspended.[1] Another way to get rid of the alt-right is to put them all in one state or give them their own country (which would be appeasement). One of the last possibilities is to actually kill them. Since none of this is going to happen, let's take a look at a speech where Milo Yiannopoulos gave steps on how to destroy the alt-right.[2]

He suggested Democrats getting rid of identity politics. Even if they did, it would not work. He said that stopping immigration would stop help stop the alt-right, but the alt-right is still going to be here, especially since whites are soon going to be the minority in America. He advised leftists to stop demonizing patriotism, but considering many on the alt-right are starting to give up on America and even conservatives say things like, "This isn't my country anymore," Yiannopoulos' advice is obviously not going to work. These, and his other ideas, are ineffective because he treats the alt-right like it's the alt-lite, just being somewhere between conservatism and race realism.

The only way to destroy the alt-right is to debate it and win, but can you convince people to leave an ideology that they don't believe is wrong or racist (and they believe they are saving the white race, which is a noble thing)? Anti-racists may celebrate when they see notable instances, like the following two, where "racists" became "anti-racists." The first is Christian Picciolini, who explained that he realized what he was doing was wrong, and then he stopped. The second is Derek Black, who grew up heavily influenced in the pro-white movement.

These two are not representative of the alt-right and even alt-righters can find it reasonable that they left the factions they were in.

Picciolini's bio says he is "a reformed extremist" from a "violent far-right hate movement" who left "the white power skinhead movement he helped build..."[3] That does not resemble the alt-right at all. They do not view themselves as being extremists, violent, far-right, hateful, into white power, or skinheads. They believe they are protecting themselves and that they hold reasonable views, and many of them abhor skinheads and almost all of the violence is not caused by the alt-right, but directed at them. It's no wonder Picciolini, an "extremist" from a "violent" movement, would leave. Even alt-righters would encourage him to (but they wouldn't want him to go as far to the left as he did). Picciolini was clearly an unstable person, and considering recent accusations of stalking, he might still be.

When it comes to Black, no wonder he had political identity problems when "He was told to be suspicious of other races, of the U.S. government, of tap water and of pop culture. His parents pulled him out of public school... when they heard his black teacher say the word 'ain't.'" These don't sound like regular people. At only thirteen, Black was getting hate mail and his parents didn't do anything about it. Later in life, he eventually started thinking that discussions "about Obama's birth certificate or DNA tests for citizenship just seemed bizarre and conspiratorial."[4] I think it's safe to say everyone in the alt-right agrees that it is bizarre.

Although anti-racists hold these two up as examples of leaving a "life of hate," almost no one in the alt-right would be convinced to leave by the same reasons Picciolini and Black were. Picciolini was, by his own admission, a part of violent extremism. Black, on the other hand, was raised by people immersing him in what could be partially called a conspiracy. The reason alt-righters won't leave for the same reasons these two did was because they believe their motives are pure.

There is an Afrikaner-only town in South Africa called Orania which, while not completely independent, has its own system of government and its own currency. How can this be if the apartheid system of South Africa was destroyed? Leftists and conservatives alike adore Nelson Mandela as a civil rights icon, but let's take a look at the South African Constitution that *he* approved. It allows "The right of self-determination of any community sharing a common cultural and language heritage..."[5] This is why an Afrikaner-only town is permissible.

So even though Picciolini and Black left their movements, alt-righters won't leave the alt-right, which they could describe as "White Zionism," any more than Israelis would abandon Zionism. The alt-right will not abandon their "right of self-determination," since even Nelson Mandela, a praised political leader, agrees that people should have self-determination.

Alt-righters see the population projections saying whites will lose massive amounts of their population while other races simultaneously gain billions. They see mass immigration into their countries leading to whites acquiring the status of minorities, while this is not happening to other countries.[6] Any excuse, any point that you try to use in a debate with them will be turned around back at other races. "Whites are becoming a minority in America, so is it okay if Mexicans become a minority in Mexico?" "Whites aren't native to America and have no rights to it? Modern Argentinians are not the natives of Argentina." "Race doesn't exist anyway? So it's okay if Mexicans become a minority in Mexico or America brings in only white immigrants?" "Whites owned slaves? There were more slaves brought to South America than the US and there are more in India *today*[7] than were brought to the US." "Whites genocided the Amerindians and owe reparations? Then Black Death genocided whites and they should get reparations." "Whites have privilege? The Chinese have privilege in China, and Asians in America make more money than whites." Anything you think of to criticize the alt-right's goals, first take it and apply it to another group and see if it makes sense. That is what they will do during a debate.

So, how do you destroy the alt-right? You can't. It believes it's right, it believes it has the moral high ground, and it's resolute. The proverbial pendulum is swinging back. Sam Dickson said, "It is fair to say... that throughout the white world, there were tens of thousands of meetings in which white people gathered to discuss how to help other races... On the same day... nowhere on the globe was there a single meeting at which non-whites met to figure out what they could do to help white people."[8] Now these meetings that whites are having are becoming meetings on how whites can save themselves. One cannot unring the bell of identitarianism. The alt-right is here, it's white, and it's not going away. It doesn't matter if the media or anyone else says white people or the alt-right are racist. The alt-right will simply reply, "We have a right to exist."[9]

Notes

Chapter 1

1. Quite literally. http://www.cnn.com/2014/11/21/tech/web/online-comment-sections/index.html

2. I do not recall which exact video I had seen, but I found one that is similar or perhaps the same.
https://www.youtube.com/watch?v=t6pzPp1Q2ew

3. Black posted this article by David Schwab Abel with a denunciation, but without denial.
https://www.stormfront.org/dblack/racist_021998.htm

4. Including the Finnish.

5. https://www.stormfront.org/forum/t579650/

6. When asked what an essential aspect of being Jewish was, "Remembering Holocaust" ranked first, with 73% of Jews acknowledging its importance.
http://www.pewforum.org/2013/10/01/jewish-american-beliefs-attitudes-culture-survey

7. http://www.timesofisrael.com/russian-speakers-who-want-to-immigrate-could-need-dna-test

8. She also stopped updating her blog.

https://www.youtube.com/user/truthisahatecrime

http://truthisahatecrime.blogspot.com

Chapter 2

1. Richard Spencer.
http://takimag.com/article/the_conservative_write#axzz4RUGQpBOe

2. Paul Gottfried. http://www.amren.com/news/2016/08/the-decline-and-rise-of-the-alternative-right

3. Donald Trump's 2013 CPAC speech.
https://www.youtube.com/watch?v=fX4wkOGqSic

4. Rosie Gray. https://www.buzzfeed.com/rosiegray/how-2015-fueled-the-rise-of-the-freewheeling-white-nationali?utm_term=.cr4nyG2mp#.ejWZ9alY3

5. Milo Yiannopoulos, Allum Bokhari.
http://www.breitbart.com/tech/2016/03/29/an-establishment-conservatives-guide-to-the-alt-right

6. They openly say this. Perhaps Yiannopoulos is talking about Chuck Johnson.

7. Maybe a handful of people might not stop at him.

8. Downvotes on both of these Youtube videos far outnumber upvotes, even though one video is posted by Hillary Clinton herself.

https://www.youtube.com/watch?v=_soeyHVrawY

https://www.youtube.com/watch?v=kHAlX9a_dfA

9. http://www.msnbc.com/the-last-word/watch/what-is-the-alt-right-movement-anyway-751089731894

10. I will discuss these videos in a later chapter.

11. Breitbart News.
https://www.youtube.com/watch?v=YeymDHht2g8

12. Sarah Posner.
http://www.motherjones.com/politics/2016/08/stephen-bannon-donald-trump-alt-right-breitbart-news

13. https://twitter.com/RosieGray/status/768891326163132416

14. https://twitter.com/PrisonPlanet/status/768915129081659394

15. https://twitter.com/vdare/status/768910827965394944

16. Although there is the theory that witnessing the Trayvon Martin/George Zimmerman incident did a *lot* when it came to turning average whites into alt-righters.

17. Sam Dickson at an NPI conference broadcasted on Red Ice TV. Minute 1:09:00. https://www.youtube.com/watch?v=gWsvBpxSXts

18. *Fash the Nation*, Week 54.
https://www.youtube.com/watch?v=vLmv0gTx4gw

19. https://www.youtube.com/watch?v=PCHJVE9trSM

Chapter 3

1. Lauren Southern's deleted tweet.
https://twitter.com/Lauren_Southern/status/802554444843982848

2. Southern is legally a male.
https://www.youtube.com/watch?v=gGpZSefYvwM

3. Due to the fact Southern put his video to "unlisted," I will not disclose the link. Contact me if you would like to see it.

4. In the video she actually sounds fascinated (read: "upset") when learning her ethnic makeup.

5. https://twitter.com/RandomlyShe/status/768813214670917632

6. Richard Spencer at an NPI conference broadcasted on Red Ice TV. Minute 1:57:00. https://www.youtube.com/watch?v=kYT3jE1Xknc

7. https://twitter.com/Lauren_Southern/status/769128779390279680

8. https://twitter.com/pnehlen/status/769018605832957953

9. Nehlen retweets John Rivers.
https://twitter.com/pnehlen/status/804209318241378304

10. https://twitter.com/pnehlen/status/804193953243418624

11. https://twitter.com/PrisonPlanet/status/755121087596355584

12. https://twitter.com/PrisonPlanet/status/769200100979707904

13. https://twitter.com/PrisonPlanet/status/798832794977771520

14. Hat tip to @Goy_Orbison.
https://twitter.com/Goy_Orbison/status/801510302718324736

15. https://twitter.com/PrisonPlanet/status/801179724768825345

16. https://twitter.com/LanaLokteff/status/801232196216487936

17. https://twitter.com/PrisonPlanet/status/801184060689170432

18. https://twitter.com/PrisonPlanet/status/801183955613532160

19. https://twitter.com/PrisonPlanet/status/801187433249468416

20. https://twitter.com/PrisonPlanet/status/801177887055298564

21. https://twitter.com/PrisonPlanet/status/801217733903974400

22. Cernovich deleted his tweet, which said "I went from libertarian to alt-right after realizing tolerance only went one way and diversity is code for white genocide." That sounds really alt-right to me. He is probably a private alt-righter while distancing himself so he can continue to sell books to people and appeal to "normies." One should also note that when his tweet was archived, it was done by someone web browsing in Japanese. Weird.

Tweet: https://twitter.com/cernovich/status/659472184679780352

Google Cache:
https://webcache.googleusercontent.com/search?q=cache:3oybw5au
gpQJ:https://twitter.com/cernovich/status/659472184679780352+&c
d=1&hl=en&ct=clnk&gl=us

Archive.org:

https://web.archive.org/web/20160815185116/https:/twitter.com/cernovich/status/659472184679780352

23. Entire article explaining how he is not alt-right, but he deleted the part where he said he wanted the alt-right to grow http://www.dangerandplay.com/2016/08/31/is-mike-cernovich-part-of-the-alt-right

https://twitter.com/Cernovich/status/776949689807622144

https://twitter.com/Cernovich/status/785152898132946944

https://twitter.com/Cernovich/status/788089901421989888

https://twitter.com/Cernovich/status/800917279357534208

It seems like only a "guilty" person would claim this many times that they are not guilty.

24. https://twitter.com/Cernovich/status/790405391528042496

25. Cernovich on Watson's Youtube channel.
https://www.youtube.com/watch?v=uWEeMYVVeBc

26. Spencer interviewed on Red Ice TV. Minute 22:00.
https://www.youtube.com/watch?v=yFaIXA-RNjI

He was discussing a number of Ann's tweets from here:

https://twitter.com/search?f=tweets&vertical=default&q=spencer%20OR%20rachel%20from%3Aanncoulter%20since%3A2016-11-22%20until%3A2016-11-23&src=typd&lang=en

27. https://twitter.com/MillennialWoes/status/802720093712977924

28. https://twitter.com/_AltRight_Anew/status/803251799859740672

29. https://twitter.com/Europa1492/status/803710152704671744

30. https://www.youtube.com/watch?v=n8HBLX_khwQ

31. https://soundcloud.com/ristofferonneberg/jared-taylor

32. https://www.youtube.com/watch?v=_YBmkGEa5-I

33. https://medium.com/mit-media-lab/who-s-influencing-election-2016-8bed68ddecc3#.3efcgd4jl

34. http://www.usatoday.com/story/tech/news/2016/11/15/twitter-suspends-alt-right-accounts/93943194

35. http://www.nydailynews.com/news/national/west-virginia-ag-spokeswoman-fired-overtly-racist-video-article-1.2766375

36. http://www.dailyrecord.co.uk/news/scottish-news/who-mystery-scottish-racist-who-9317228

37. If you'd just read a little further you'll see what it means.

38. http://www.riverfronttimes.com/newsblog/2016/10/14/st-louis-native-trashes-city-as-uninhabitable-hellhole-reveals-self-as-racist-moron

39. http://forward.com/news/national/355592/politico-editor-michael-hirsch-resigns-after-threatening-white-nationalist

40. https://www.youtube.com/watch?v=2VOB6_Xt2P4

41. http://nypost.com/2016/12/05/phillies-pistachio-girl-fired-for-being-avowed-white-nationalist

42. https://archive.org/details/cuckilini

43. https://www.youtube.com/watch?v=eQprOAGzotE

44. https://medium.com/@recnepss/does-love-really-live-here-fff159563ba3#.ucilsqhfo

45. Since writing this Nehlen has did a Reddit AMA (Ask Me Anything) chat for fans on alt-right Reddit.

https://www.reddit.com/r/altright/comments/5haqvj/ama_tonight_ill_be_there_at_830_et_finishing_up_a

46. Youtube deleted the video "for violating YouTube's policy on hate speech." https://www.youtube.com/watch?v=QiicA2tuEHU It was later uploaded to Vimeo. https://vimeo.com/194237858 It was then reuploaded with the racial slurs bleeped out.
https://www.youtube.com/watch?v=J7dIZmHiEoQ

47. Spencer interviewed on Red Ice TV. Minute 24:00.
https://www.youtube.com/watch?v=yFalXA-RNjI

48. https://www.youtube.com/watch?v=G74sCg_n9rY

49. I'm joking.

50. https://www.youtube.com/watch?v=JPnZa1FHcN4

51. https://www.youtube.com/watch?v=wOmSxGoYGeY

52. https://www.youtube.com/watch?v=q8dqK-N5600

53. https://www.youtube.com/watch?v=3rnRPhEwELo

54. https://www.youtube.com/watch?v=CJ3B6L2fUA8

Chapter 4

1. http://www.counter-currents.com/2012/06/frequently-asked-questions-part-1

2. Tom Swiss. http://www.patheos.com/blogs/thezenpagan/2016/11/ethnic-pride-vs-white-nationalism

3. https://www.youtube.com/watch?v=J3B85zur1jA

4. https://twitter.com/_AltRight_Anew/status/802008752949956608

5. Ann Coulter on Hannity. http://www.breitbart.com/video/2016/11/15/ann-coulter-appropriate-reaction-calling-bannon-anti-semitic-racist-screw

6. https://www.youtube.com/watch?v=GS-yO91PCCU

7. The title tag of Anthony Browne's piece is "Non-whites will be majority in US and Europe by 2050." https://www.theguardian.com/uk/2000/sep/03/race.world Note, some estimates differ and there are a few exceptions. If you would like to do your own research, just search each white country individually, estimate the amount of people lost due to the current total fertility rate, subtract that, add immigrants who are primarily non-white, and make an estimation over the next thirty-three years, for a result for 2050 (for Browne's claim). Then, if the country still has a white

113

majority, just go another fifty years to 2100, a year many alt-righters use, and you will find it to be a white minority country.

8. http://www.bls.gov/cps/cpsaat18.htm

9. Jonathan Adams. http://www.colorlines.com/articles/dreadful-genius-obama-moment

10. https://twitter.com/NathanDamigo/status/803558126163103744

11. Spencer at an NPI conference broadcasted on Red Ice TV. Minute 4:03:00. https://www.youtube.com/watch?v=kYT3jE1Xknc

12. Ronnie Polaneczky. http://www.philly.com/philly/news/politics/dnc/20160727_Disabled_finally_have_a_place_at_the_DNC.html

Chapter 5

1. http://www.salon.com/2015/09/21/im_a_pedophile_but_not_a_monster

2. http://www.slate.com/articles/news_and_politics/jurisprudence/2004/01/vile_vile_pedophile.html

3. There is such a thing as "willing" something into existence. "Memeing" something into existence is repeatedly using something over and over on the Internet or virtual realm that it eventually materializes into the physical world (or gains the attention of the

physical world) and has real life consequences. Example: The alt-right memed Trump into the White House.

4. http://www.adl.org/combating-hate/hate-on-display/c/pepe-the-frog.html

5. F Roger Devlin at an NPI conference broadcasted on Red Ice TV. Minute 6:07:00. https://www.youtube.com/watch?v=kYT3jE1Xknc

6. Example:

> Person 1 writes on the Internet, "I saw (((Natalie Portman))) yesterday at the store. (((She))) was picking a penny up off the floor."

> Person 2 sees the parentheses and the penny comment, and then writes "You don't need to repeat yourself."

7. Wyand is a Twitterer with over 134k followers and he came to prominence by being a vocal supporter of Trump. He used to either block or fight against people who were "racist" and "anti-Semitic" on Twitter, but not after the echo arrived.
https://twitter.com/JaredWyand/status/800554260131958784

8. http://www.adl.org/combating-hate/hate-on-display/c/echo.html

9. Adele Stan. http://www.alternet.org/election-2016/7-demeaning-alt-right-terms-used-racist-trump-followers

10. The cuckoo bird lays its egg in the nest of a reed warbler bird, it hatches and kicks the reed warbler eggs out to their doom, and the reed warbler thinks the cuckoo is its own offspring. It feeds it

115

constantly even when the cuckoo grows to FIVE TIMES the reed warbler's size. "Cuckold" is an archaic term ("cuck" is the modern term) describing a man whose wife had sex with another man. There is a category of porn about cuckolds wherein they primarily feature a white man getting "cucked" by a black man, hence racial connotations. "Cuck" and "cuckservative" means a conservative who is a sellout, like a "RINO" (Republican In Name Only), or it is used by the alt-right to mean a politician who is not alt-right and who is selling out his race, a man who is raising the children of another man, or basically any Christian who gives charity to foreigners (I say Christian because they are the main ones doing that):

11. Glenn Beck meets most definitions of "cuckservative." http://www.glennbeck.com/2016/10/28/learn-and-reject-the-alt-rights-language

12. Someone even made a Youtube video questioning whether or not Barron has autism, but then deleted it and claimed Melania Trump threatened to sue. http://dailycaller.com/2016/11/28/someone-alleged-that-barron-trump-is-autistic-now-melania-trump-is-firing-back

13. The Right Stuff's alt-right lexicon. http://therightstuff.biz/trs-lexicon

14. There are other definitions and types of "autistes," but the rest are not relevant to alt-rightism.

15. If your memes are especially fashy or autistic, Ann Coulter will retweet you. Few know this. She has retweeted (and follows) memer "Can't Stump the Trump" multiple times, such as

https://twitter.com/CantStumpTrump1/status/804050225514024961 on November 30, and she retweeted https://twitter.com/FashyMemetics/status/802904547832238080 on November 28.

16. Rick Wilson on MSNBC.
https://www.youtube.com/watch?v=MqMtXHwrG4o

17. Rick Wilson on MSNBC. https://www.youtube.com/watch?v=_tj-Hp7AYlk

18.
https://twitter.com/MerriamWebster/status/803674255732813825

19. Mike Ma was suspended from Twitter, so this https://twitter.com/mikema_/status/763907281100607488 is gone, but Google still has its cache: https://webcache.googleusercontent.com/search?q=cache:sHowKJkQ T7QJ:https://twitter.com/mikema_/status/763907281100607488+&cd =1&hl=en&ct=clnk&gl=us

20. Audra Schroeder. http://www.dailydot.com/unclick/real-taylor-swift-pinterest-quotes-hitler

21. It has been said that harassment led to the deletion. https://www.pinterest.com/piratemily

22. True story.

23. Fruzsina Eordogh actually fell for this. http://www.forbes.com/sites/fruzsinaeordogh/2016/06/02/explaining -the-sam-hyde-as-mass-shooter-meme

24. Allum Bokhari. http://www.breitbart.com/tech/2015/12/22/ben-garrison-how-the-internet-made-a-fake-white-supremacist

25. https://twitter.com/scrowder/status/687260244364267522

26. https://twitter.com/search?f=images&vertical=default&q=alt%20right%20crowder&src=typd

27. David Duke on *Fash the Nation*, Week 59. Minute 1:48:00. https://www.youtube.com/watch?v=37VQ03u9OAw

28. Monica Hesse, Dan Zak. https://www.washingtonpost.com/news/arts-and-entertainment/wp/2016/11/30/does-this-haircut-make-me-look-like-a-nazi

29. Sinead McCarthy. https://twitter.com/Sineaderade/status/805859225318592514

30. "Trump Train Can't Stop 'We Can't Stop' by Miley Cyrus Parody." https://www.youtube.com/watch?v=khMwEVik_xc

31. https://twitter.com/BecomeWhoWeAre/status/805750286199427072

32. "IQ Tests" by Walt Bismarck. https://www.youtube.com/watch?v=JWzjn0N9g4g

33. "Love is a Giant Wall" by Walt Bismarck. https://www.youtube.com/watch?v=L5lpLHaVXnM

34. The real leader of the alt-right. https://twitter.com/BronzeAgePerv

35. Walt Bismarck's "We Didn't Start The Movement." The original was blocked in America.
https://www.youtube.com/watch?v=21wxkpk27FY

Chapter 6

1. The blog, Altright-Watch, did a great job of compiling and explaining the entire event. http://altright-watch.blogspot.com/2016/11/live-npis-become-who-we-are-2016.html

2. https://www.youtube.com/watch?v=wlbLNWIFEY0

3. https://twitter.com/BrandonToddFOX4/status/806297066418958336

4. https://twitter.com/ralphhaurwitz/status/806298725773615105

5. Don't ask them one or they might convert you.

6. Face it, she's better at animation.

7. https://www.youtube.com/watch?v=faNge-o0V-k

8. https://www.youtube.com/watch?v=lKDeyuM0-Og

9. Not actual quote.

10. This is what I imagine him as.

11. http://www.ohchr.org/EN/ProfessionalInterest/Pages/CrimeOfGenocide.aspx

An alt-righter would say that taxing whites at the expense of them having children and giving the money to non-whites to support their children fits this description of genocide and results in literally having whites pay to replace themselves. I will explain more about births in the next chapter, but if you insist people *choose* whether or not to have enough children to sustain the population, an alt-righter would point out that government incentives and disincentives can provably increase or decrease the total fertility rate.

Chapter 7

1. The main character in *The Matrix* had the choice to take the red pill to wake up out of the virtual reality and see the harsh, real world, or take the blue pill to remain comfy and oblivious to the real world. Meninists, pick-up artists, etc. used the term to refer to men who "woke up" and realized feminists were taking over society. The alt-right then commandeered the term.

2. http://www.radixjournal.com/the-red-pill

3. http://ec.europa.eu/eurostat/statistics-explained/index.php/Fertility_statistics

4. https://www.cia.gov/library/publications/the-world-factbook/rankorder/2127rank.html

5. Paul Bedard. http://www.washingtonexaminer.com/census-whites-become-minority-in-2044-hispanic-population-twice-blacks/article/2557393

6. Doug Ware.
http://www.upi.com/Top_News/US/2015/03/05/Census-White-children-to-become-minority-by-2020/9751425612082

7. Rosa Silverman.
http://www.telegraph.co.uk/news/uknews/immigration/10032296/White-Britons-will-be-minority-by-2066-says-professor.html

8. Lizzie Dearden. http://www.independent.co.uk/news/uk/home-news/muhammed-really-is-most-popular-baby-name-in-the-uk-as-is-mohammed-muhammad-9895605.html

9. http://www.therightperspective.org/2010/08/12/8-percent-of-us-newborns-are-anchor-babies

10. If you assume 100% are Hispanics. It should be at least 75% Hispanic.

11. Whites are 62% of the US and 49% of the births. In California, whites are 38% and only 28% of births.

38%: http://www.census.gov/quickfacts/table/PST045215/06

28%: http://www.kidsdata.org/topic/31/births-race/table#fmt=146&loc=2&tf=73&ch=7,11,8,507,9,73,74&sortColumnId=0&sortType=asc

12. Anderson Cooper and Ray Nagin on CNN.
https://www.youtube.com/watch?v=QEH9u26Vlhk

13. Matthew Yglesias.
http://www.slate.com/blogs/moneybox/2012/12/13/the_plan_is_real_there_is_a_plan_to_eradicate_dc_s_black_majority_and_it.html

14. Courtland Milloy. https://www.washingtonpost.com/local/for-ivy-city-the-plan-isnt-paranoia/2012/12/11/7ab31660-43de-11e2-9648-a2c323a991d6_story.html

15. https://www.youtube.com/watch?v=1XDWn0Q7tqg

16. https://twitter.com/theeagle/status/806231941167063044

17. https://www.youtube.com/watch?v=V054eqVFaXs

18. Daniel Solomon reporting on Matt Rosenberg. http://forward.com/news/national/356363/speechless-rabbi-admits-losing-argument-over-racism-and-israel-to-white-sup

19. FBI, 2012. https://ucr.fbi.gov/crime-in-the-u.s/2012/crime-in-the-u.s.-2012/offenses-known-to-law-enforcement/expanded-homicide/expanded_homicide_data_table_6_murder_race_and_sex_of_vicitm_by_race_and_sex_of_offender_2012.xls

20. Criminal Victimization in the United States, 2005 Statistical Tables, Page 55. http://www.bjs.gov/content/pub/pdf/cvus05.pdf

21. Personally, I think someone fell asleep at the computer and made a mistake. 100%? Really?

22. http://paultown.com/white-vs-black-crime

23. https://twitter.com/Third_Position/status/800218198851235840

24. Steve Sailer. http://isteve.blogspot.com/2014/03/2008-sat-scores-by-race-by-income.html

25. Time preference can be explained basically by telling a child they can have a candy bar now, or two in an hour. It's whether or not

people work hard now and postpone reward for later (when it is worth more). https://en.wikipedia.org/wiki/Time_preference

26. Jared Taylor on the Darwin Digest. Minute 54. https://soundcloud.com/darwin-digest/episode-24-a-chat-with-jared-taylor

27. I can't actually find any written examples, but I remember hearing (in either videos or podcasts, and one Twitter conversation) at least four alt-righters saying that this specific event led them to becoming alt-right.

28. Tim Wise. http://www.dailykos.com/story/2010/11/3/916577/-

29. https://www.youtube.com/watch?v=6BnbwUT7lBg

30. https://www.youtube.com/watch?v=z6llGoeDIUQ

31. https://www.youtube.com/watch?v=kcM3k5KrYjE

32. Paul Bedard. http://www.washingtonexaminer.com/black-law-editor-acquit-anyone-charged-with-murdering-raping-whites/article/2609148

33. Symone Sanders. https://www.youtube.com/watch?v=g5ulvcqaiM8

34. http://dailycaller.com/2016/11/26/keith-ellison-once-proposed-making-a-separate-country-for-blacks

35. http://www.vdare.com/posts/zero-black-congressmen-disavow-keith-ellisons-plan-for-a-black-ethnostate

36. https://twitter.com/AC360/status/804131194065584128

37. Keith Lamont Scott's brother.

https://www.youtube.com/watch?v=5zxMrXsEzPs

38. https://www.youtube.com/watch?v=YlB9bwQBBCk

39. http://www.alternet.org/news-amp-politics/yes-all-white-people-are-racists-now-lets-do-something-about-it

40. http://www.newsbusters.org/blogs/nb/justin-mccarthy/2008/03/24/joy-behar-oppressed-minorities-cant-be-racist

41. http://www.huffingtonpost.ca/marni-soupcoff/cbc-caucasian-ad-job-posting_b_3185940.html

42. Canadian Broadcasting Corporation.

https://www.youtube.com/watch?v=Wb55teb1gJ0

43. https://www.youtube.com/watch?v=BnC56tmHh9Q

44. Google's 2014 Diversity Statistics.

https://googleblog.blogspot.com/2014/05/getting-to-work-on-diversity-at-google.html

45. RamZPaul. https://www.youtube.com/watch?v=DZIEk2Edt4g

46. Google's 2016 Diversity Statistics.

https://www.google.com/diversity

47. Totals do not equal 100% because "Two or more races" and "Other" were not included. Here they are... 2014: Two or more races 4%, Other <1%. 2016: Two or more races 3%, Other <1%.

Chapter 8

1. Brett Stevens. http://www.amerika.org/politics/no-the-alt-right-is-not-dead-white-nationalism-is

2. He actually said it was Richard Spencer's first goal. https://twitter.com/mattklewis/status/806499649314029568

3. Minute 17. https://www.youtube.com/watch?v=G74sCg_n9rY

4. https://twitter.com/search?f=tweets&vertical=default&q=congress%20from%3Arichardbspencer%20since%3A2016-12-16%20until%3A2016-12-20&src=typd

5. Kevin MacDonald. http://www.theoccidentalobserver.net/2016/08/will-the-alt-right-take-over-the-republican-party

6. Ben Shapiro. https://www.washingtonpost.com/posteverything/wp/2016/08/18/the-breitbart-alt-right-just-took-over-the-gop

7. Minute 41. http://www.counter-currents.com/2016/11/introducing-identity-europa

8. Andrew Anglin. http://www.dailystormer.com/how-to-be-a-nigger-on-twitter

9. https://www.reddit.com/r/altright/comments/5g6jz5/ask_iron_mitten_anything

10. https://www.youtube.com/watch?v=Z-7EOagzsTc

More info: https://www.youtube.com/watch?v=qrybz26uk10

11. http://altright-watch.blogspot.com/2016/10/identity-evropa-protest-live-stream.html

12. Matt Tait at the 2015 American Renaissance conference. Minute 17:00. https://www.youtube.com/watch?v=Zo2MD-Ou7AQ

13. Look at the comment section of The Young Turks' interview with Nathan Damigo. People are even making sexual innuendos about him. https://www.youtube.com/watch?v=muf3XYTXfHk

14. Mona Chalabi. http://fivethirtyeight.com/datalab/how-many-times-the-average-person-moves

15. Pema Levy. http://talkingpointsmemo.com/dc/trump-let-in-more-white-immigrants

16. Joy Reid. https://twitter.com/JoyAnnReid/status/771172246102519809

17. Minute 10. https://www.youtube.com/watch?v=NKkbxFXRedc

18. I had to keep chopping out parts of the article to make the point concise and avoid the risk of copyright infringement, but you should just read the whole thing: http://www.counter-currents.com/2014/06/the-slow-cleanse

Chapter 9

1. On 12/10/16 (about a month after being suspended).

2. https://www.youtube.com/watch?v=wNRGW1VtPJE

3. http://www.christianpicciolini.com/bio

4. Eli Saslow. https://www.washingtonpost.com/national/the-white-flight-of-derek-black/2016/10/15/ed5f906a-8f3b-11e6-a6a3-d50061aa9fae_story.html

5. Page 121 or 125, depending on how you count. http://www.justice.gov.za/legislation/constitution/SAConstitution-web-eng.pdf

More reading on the topic: http://www.justice.gov.za/legislation/constitution/history/INTERIM/TCR/ACCORD.PDF

https://www.nelsonmandela.org/omalley/index.php/site/q/03lv02039/04lv02103/05lv02120/06lv02123.htm

6. Maybe a couple (which leftists decry as genocide).

7. http://assets.globalslaveryindex.org/downloads/Global+Slavery+Index+2016.pdf

8. Sam Dickson at the 2011 NPI conference. Minute 7. https://www.youtube.com/watch?v=UidMZluvlfY

9. If you would like to be philosophical and say, "No, you don't," then an alt-righter might ask, "So you're okay with someone killing *you* because you don't have the right to exist anyway?"